THE NON
RELIGIOUS
CHRISTIAN

THE NON RELIGIOUS CHRISTIAN

FINDING FAITH OUTSIDE THE CHURCH

VERN JONES

PRINCIPIA
MEDIA

Wyoming, Michigan

© 2012 Vern Jones
Published by Principia Media, LLC, Wyoming, MI
www. principiamedia.com

ISBN-13: 978-1-61485-002-1

Principia Media, LLC
1853 R W Berends Drive SW
Wyoming, MI 49519

Scripture quotations, unless otherwise indicated, are taken from the HOLY BIBLE, NEW INTERNATIONAL VERSION®. NIV®. Copyright ©1973, 1978, 1984 by International Bible Society. Used by permission of Zondervan. All rights reserved.

Scripture quotations marked KJV are taken from the Holy Bible, King James Version, Cambridge, 1769.

Printed in the United States of America

17 16 15 14 13 12   7 6 5 4 3 2 1

Cover Design: Revel www.revel.in
Interior Layout: Virginia McFadden

Dedication

To Irene, my wife and best friend,
who has combined constant
encouragement, motivation and support,
with a love I never believed was possible.

To my children Adam, Kati, Jill, Julie and Kristin,
whose questions and challenges motivated me
to put these thoughts into words.

To my father Harry and my mother Thelma,
for giving me a solid foundation
and a living example of an enduring faith.

To Grandpa Linderman,
who allowed me to question a faith
that sustained him through an incredible life
and encouraged me to find a faith that I could own.

To the memory of a dear friend, Dave Kloppe,
whose coffee shop conversations were the basis
for much of this book.

Acknowledgments

The writing and publishing of this book would not have happened without the invaluable assistance of several people to whom I will be eternally indebted.

Shortly after the completion of the first draft of my manuscript I had the great fortune of meeting Dirk Wierenga. His skills as a content editor helped me refine my message well beyond my initial efforts, and his knowledge of the publishing industry helped me avoid some serious mistakes common to first-time authors. Without his guidance and hands-on assistance, Principia Media would not exist. Within the course of a year, Dirk has gone from acquaintance to editor, to confidant, to partner, and finally, a deeply-trusted friend. My wife and I are truly grateful for all his hard work and confidence.

I am deeply grateful for the undying support and encouragement from my wife Irene who has been my greatest supporter of this controversial book. She has remained steadfast in spite of opposition from our predominantly evangelical friends and neighbors. Her encouragement and fresh coffee, along with the cold nose of our dog Mika, consistently enticed me to arise early from a warm bed to complete this project.

I would like to thank our daughter Julie Hurley for her careful editing, comments, and fact checking which make me appear a much better writer than I really am.

I would also like to thank Tracey, Jason and the staff at Revel for their professional and creative work on this book cover as well as the wonderful website development for Principia Media, www.principiamedia.com.

And lastly, I would like to thank the wonderful staff at Principia Media for not only their efforts in the publication of this book, but in their commitment to provide a national voice for new and emerging authors whose work support the goals of living a Meaningful Life.

Contents

Foreword

Many persons undergo a process of growth and change in their religious views as they progress through life. It is rare for a person to document the reasons for that development. Vern Jones does just that. He was raised in a conservative Baptist home, which meant that he was raised in the church and on the Bible. Immersed in both water and Biblical knowledge, he began asking questions about the Bible at a very early age. He was rebuffed by his pastor but gently and reverently encouraged by a kindly grandfather. He came to doubt that the Bible was the inerrant word of God. As an adult, although he is a scientist, he continued to study biblical scholarship. In this book he unfolds the process by which he documented these early suspicions.

It is Jones' conclusion that the story of Jesus as told in the Bible was from very early on drafted into the service of a religious orthodoxy that eclipsed the real teaching of Jesus. He traces the negative impact of this from the compilation of the New Testament through the two thousand years of the history of the church. Citing the subjugation of the teaching of Jesus to the interests of the Roman Empire, the crusades, and inquisition, Jones details how the church strayed dramatically from the simple instruction of Jesus. In American history he sees a similar phenomenon. From the Salem witch trials to the contemporary suppression of homosexuals, the church has co-opted the Bible in the service of slavery, racism, war and politics. The church has consistently questioned the developments of science and fostered ignorance, especially in rejecting the theory of evolution in recent times. Thus having found the church guilty by the very teachings of Jesus, Jones opted out of the church altogether.

But the story takes a surprising turn. While attempting to extract the central message of Jesus, Jones became a more ardent disciple. He became what he calls a "non-religious Christian," finding faith outside the church. The dynamics of his faith comes from the post-crucifixion experience of the disciples. Something turned them from a group of cowards to fearless advocates of the way of life taught by Jesus. Jones concludes that this dramatic change is evidence of the resurrection of Jesus. "This allows one," he suggests, "to see the teachings of Christ without the dogma of religion. By doing so one will experience the greatest teacher to ever walk the Earth, and, in the process, to rediscover a loving God." (p. 174) This challenges us to a life of morality characterized by love of neighbor, to "be better than we believe possible." (p.178)

The millions of Americans who have been raised in a restrictive religious environment and who have wrestled with these issues will find this book extremely helpful. Some have remained in church or found a more compatible congregation while some have become atheists, and some have been mired down in between. I went through a very similar development. I started in life as a conservative Southern Baptist minister. For a long while I too dropped out of the church. My development brought me back into the pulpit as a Presbyterian minister. My choice was to bring the dynamic teaching of Jesus back into the church itself, and from there to help transform the church into a dynamic Christ force in our society rather than a prop support for the immoral and unchristian status quo.

Jones' book will be extremely valuable to many who will not have the time or energy to resolve these issues in an exhaustive manner. The great strength and power of Jones' work stems in part from the fact that he is a layperson. He writes not in the stilted language of those trained in theology or Biblical studies, but in the language of the heart and gut. He writes with the logic of a scientist and the earnestness and passion of a true disciple. He is to be commended for sharing this pilgrimage with us.

Fred J. Hood
Presbyterian Minister and Author
(*Reformed America*, 1982, 2002; *Steps to Spiritual Growth*, 2004;
Religious Right and Right Religion, 2012)
Founder and Chairman Emeritus of Shepherd's House
Lexington, KY

Introduction

They Don't Make Christians
Like Grandpa Anymore

I was raised in a Christian home by parents and grandparents who were wonderful examples of how to live a Christ-centered life. At the head of our household was my grandfather, Harold Linderman.

Grandpa was an exceptional man who possessed a subtle yet understated humor. He was fond of telling everyone that he graduated in the top ten of his high school class; on the 13th of June; in 1913; in a class of thirteen students. This in an era when most people left school before the eighth grade.

As a rural route postal carrier, my grandfather delivered mail by horse and buggy. To help feed our extended family, Grandpa also ran a maintenance farm with milk cows, chickens, pigs, a couple of horses, and some beef cattle. I can still remember him hand milking the cows on his one-legged stool, occasionally squirting the fresh milk into the mouths of our barn cats. Our farm was known for having the best red raspberries in the area which we hand-picked and sold beside the road on an honors system.

Grandpa was a devout Christian. As lifetime members of our local Baptist church, my grandparents drove our family three miles both ways to attend each service. Let me emphasize, *every* service. Baptists love to keep the church busy. Services started early in the morning with Sunday school followed by worship which lasted until noon. After church, we returned home to complete our farm chores while Grandma and Mother made dinner. Following a huge meal, we would play checkers or work on a jig-saw puzzle before changing into our church clothes again and driving back for the evening services followed by youth Bible study.

For us, church was an everyday event. Tuesday night was youth night; midweek worship was held Wednesday night; Thursday was Bible study; Friday featured guest preachers and traveling evangelists. It was a schedule my parents enforced for all five siblings that lasted until I left home for college.

For my grandfather our busy church schedule was not what made him a Christian, nor did it define him. Growing up, living on my grandparent's farm, I had a great opportunity to witness my grandpa live a Christ-like life on a daily basis.

My parents married after my father returned from serving in Europe during WWII. Like most returning veterans, they had very little money. My father worked in a factory twenty miles away and had to leave home early each morning and returned late in the day. Once home he helped Grandpa with the farm chores.

Our family lived in a 450-square-foot outbuilding behind my grandparent's house, which was later converted to a garage. Because we had no running water, we ate most of our meals with my grandparents. We were not their only borders. Grandpa and Grandma also assumed the responsibilities for raising any relatives that were unwanted, unruly, or simply liked it better at their home. Over the years, by my mother's count, fourteen relatives lived in their home at one time or another.

Growing up, under the watchful eye of various Sunday school teachers, I read the Bible from cover to cover numerous times. Frequent church-sponsored contests were held with prizes offered to those who memorized the names of the books of the Bible and specific verses. There was also an annual award presented to everyone who read the entire Bible. Since we had little money, and the prizes were quite impressive, I made a point of winning as many as possible.

In addition to memorization, my parents, grandparents, and many of my aunts and uncles practiced devotions which involved reading at least one chapter of the Bible each night after supper. It is not an exaggeration to say that I became very familiar with the King James Bible.

At the same time, like many children, from the time I could read I was infatuated with dinosaurs and the unusual creatures disclosed by the extensive fossil records. This infatuation led to my first conflict between science and religion. If the Bible was an historical record from the creation of man to the present, why was there no mention of these magnificent creatures? Certainly they would have posed a significant challenge to Noah or the nomadic journeys of the Israelites. Every question of this nature was deferred by my parents to the ultimate authority in our church community, Pastor Demorest.

Pastor Demorest was a large man with a booming, intimidating voice who had an explanation for everything biblical. He often used an explanation that Satan had obviously planted the bones to distract man from the truth of God's creation. That answer satisfied my nine-year-old curiosity. After all, I was taught nearly from birth that we were constantly being tempted by Satan; who tempted us to dance, to listen to rock and roll music, to gamble, to play card games, and drink alcohol.

My teenage years were filled with more questions, and each time Pastor Demorest predictably blamed not only the devil but also me for my wavering faith. As he explained, I should simply believe because God wants some things to remain a mystery. He then instructed me to return to the Bible for answers and to renew my faith by simply praying for God's guidance in my search.

During those formative years my only reliable resource was Grandpa. When posed with the fossil record conflict, Grandpa simply said that he had a problem with that too. Later he came to the conclusion that one day of creation was an immeasurable amount of time and not a day in the conventional sense. Grandpa went on to say it was possible that God created different animals at different times over a very long period. Some animals survived, and others didn't. In Grandpa's mind, the dinosaurs did not survive the Great Flood, because Noah certainly would have mentioned their inclusion. It was his modified version of the evolution of animals and natural selection, although he would never have used those words as they directly contradicted his beloved religion. Grandpa explained that sometimes you have to resolve biblical conflicts within your own mind because the Bible does not mean the same thing to everyone. While he respected the beliefs of Pastor Demorest, he did not let them control his own thoughts.

Those discussions with Grandpa created endless possibilities and gave me permission to challenge established church dogma and led me on a quest to discover the essence of the Bible.

My Baptist faith, like that of many fundamentalist Christians, believed that every word in the Bible was directly inspired by God and therefore the Bible was without error. Since each word was dictated by God, this allowed pastors to dissect every phrase, sentence structure, and indeed every word as being a message directly from God. I once heard a preacher give an entire sermon on one word in the Bible, and why God chose that word above all others. The fact that my grandfather, a pillar and deacon in the church, believed there was room for interpretation gave me license to use my God-given intelligence and logic to find a Christianity that I could believe.

As Grandpa grew into his seventies, I recall asking him what he thought about the incredible claim in the Bible that Methuselah lived to the age of 969 years.

Grandpa responded in his predictably honest way, "I don't know." He quickly added that as he got older, and his mobility became more limited, he couldn't imagine wanting to live that long. Grandpa observed that he had outlived his father and grandfather due to the advances of modern medicine and a much-improved diet. Without penicillin and vaccines, he acknowledged, it seemed unlikely that someone could live to be that old.

I could see that Grandpa struggled with his undying belief that the Bible was the Word of God. He reasoned that a year had a different time frame than we use today. He concluded, as he always did, by encouraging me to look into it and ultimately to decide for myself.

Grandpa would never share with me his greatest concerns with the Bible, as he didn't want to plant doubt about a God and religion that had brought him comfort. Instead he encouraged me to take ownership of my beliefs and to personally explore, question, and discern where God leads me. I distinctly recall his advice, "God gave us wonderful minds, use yours to find your peace in Him."

My grandpa was careful to always remind me that the answers he found were not the "truth" but simply conclusions he reached using the logic and information he had at that time. He explained that in many instances additional questions arose, or new information presented itself. This often caused him to become uncomfortable with his own beliefs. This state of being uncomfortable was never relieved by stubbornly sticking to an entrenched conclusion. It was and is important to explore the question, do more research and open one's heart to receive God's guidance to find inner peace.

Grandpa explained that comfort does not come to us from the pulpit or a book; it comes to us through our own faith.

Over the years, Grandpa and I discussed many stories from the Bible, often while picking raspberries. He loved the flow of the language in the King James Bible. When I asked him his favorite verse, he didn't hesitate for a second. "My favorite is the same of many Christians—John 3:16," he explained. "It's a wonderful promise from Christ that the only condition for eternal life is to believe in him. While he provides a lot of guidance for a full and abundant life, the grace of God alone is what allows us to see God in all his splendor." That is the God my grandpa believed in; a God who doesn't require a groveling servant, no intermediaries, no pleas for money, or acts of attrition. His was simply a pure faith.

It was clear from our conversations that another favorite passage was not really a verse, but a series of statements called the Beatitudes, which are found in both Matthew and Luke. Those beautiful promises and blessings obviously provided Grandpa great comfort.

For me, the eight Beatitude blessings attributed to Jesus have become my favorites as well. I remember the comfort they gave me when Grandpa told me how those verses applied to his own life. Even though we were quite poor, those verses told me that I was blessed even though we didn't have many of the things other kids had. That was all right. Jesus told me I was blessed.

The discussion with Grandpa I cherish most began with a simple question I asked while eating the raspberries we were picking, "How do you know there is a God?"

Grandpa paused, placed a beautiful red raspberry in his mouth and relished the simple sweetness. "He talks to me. Not in a loud booming voice but quietly when I am all alone. God tells me the moral, ethical path with this silent unwavering voice in the back of my head." I asked if he meant his conscience. He softly corrected, "My Holy Spirit."

My life, my faith, and my perception of Grandpa changed with each conversation. They helped me find my faith, my God, my comfort, and to continue to follow my Holy Spirit.

Later on I learned to appreciate the influence Grandpa had within our small community when, one day, I visited him in the hospital. He had fallen out of an apple tree and crushed his heel. When I entered his room he was reading the Bible. I asked, "What were you doing in an apple tree? You are eighty-one years old." His response was typical Grandpa, "That's where the apples are." I asked if there was anything I could do to help, other than help Grandma with the house and farm. He said that he was worried for the old people in town whose lawns he mowed weekly. At eighty-one years, he was taking care of the elderly, some of whom were years younger than he, and refused to take more than two dollars for gas.

Grandpa lived the Christian life every day and every hour for his entire ninety-six years. He was not a saint and was not perfect, but he was the Christian I aspire to be. Grandpa is with me every day. I see him in acts of kindness, in the silliness of my grandchildren, and in the smile in my wife's eyes.

It saddens me to think there are some in the church who say that people who have beliefs like my grandpa are not Christian. He was the most influential person in my early life and the one I am most indebted to for the foundation of my own faith.

Though some may say that I have wandered from the true spirit of Christianity, through my studies I have found two core beliefs: I know there is a God; and I believe Christ was sent by God to show us the path to human fulfillment.

At the same time I do not believe many of the stories found in the Bible and reject much of the dogma professed by certain Christian denominations. As he has for over two-thousand years, I know that Christ changes lives every day and that my life has been blessed as a result.

While my beliefs may differ from others, I am comfortable living out my faith exemplified by my grandfather.

I consider myself a Christian without the burdens found in organized religion. My beliefs can be summed up by the author of Luke who writes in chapter 17: 20–21, *"The kingdom of God does not come with your careful observation, nor will people say, 'Here it is,' or 'There it is,' because the kingdom of God is within you."*

Thanks, Grandpa.

PART ONE
The Inerrancy of the Bible

1

Our Inspired, Inerrant, and Literal Bible

Like many, I struggle with inconsistencies and inaccuracies within the Bible. I also wonder if the Bible was directly dictated by God to a chosen few.

Depending on the Christian denomination, God either dictated each word without error or it was written by humans with divinely inspired hands. Growing up, my minister liked to say that God used the hands of the authors to write these precious Scriptures.

My belief in God would certainly allow for such behavior if God were so inclined. However, my reading of Scripture makes this very difficult for me to believe. Taking a closer look at the content of the Bible one might reasonably conclude that if God actually did move the hands of the writers then his work would be perfect, without flaw or, in a word, inerrant. Anything less would be flawed, imperfect or not Godlike. If, through evaluations and discussion of the Bible, we detect any flaws or inconsistencies we would be forced to conclude it was not dictated by God. Or, God is not perfect, or, possibly, that God placed these errors intentionally in the Bible to confuse or challenge us.

The belief that God inspired each word is critical in nearly every Christian theology. From Catholics to Baptists it is common to end the reading of Scripture with "this is the Word of God."

But as I read from both the Old and New Testaments there appear to be errors and significant inconsistencies.

The very notion of questioning some passages in the Bible may be difficult for some to confront or may even sound blasphemous. My purpose is to challenge the inerrancy of Scripture, not the existence of God. To me they are not the same. Like John Lennon challenged us in his song—to imagine a world with no religion. It doesn't mean there are no Christian values or God does not exist, it simply means no organized religion. It's a difficult challenge. I challenge you to think of Christianity—the belief and worship of Jesus the Christ—without your religion.

I don't believe in the inerrancy of the Bible. I do believe that the authors were motivated by their love of God and that the truth we desire is based on much of the writing found in the Bible.

As Christians we base our beliefs on the Bible just as the Hindu believe in the Bhagavad Gita, the Muslims in the Koran, the Jews in the Torah, and the Taoists in the Tao-te-ching. All of these sacred books profess to be direct messages from God which profess to be the only way to eternal happiness. Which of these is correct? Can each faith be true to God while believing in separate teachings? Is there only one way to God?

Perhaps church leaders fear it would be more difficult to convert non-believers if they claimed the Bible is "pretty close" to the truth. Common wisdom says providing wiggle room may be a pretty weak sales pitch to potential converts. Every religion claims its holy book provides the only truth. Selling a religion and creating converts requires a claim of absolute truth and the only path to eternal bliss, just as a manufacturer claims their product is better than the competition.

Scripture is filled with claims of inerrancy. Psalm 12:6 *"And the words of the Lord are flawless, like silver refined in a furnace of clay, purified seven times."* Proverbs 30:5 *"Every word of God is flawless."* 2 Timothy 3:16 *"All Scripture is God-breathed and is useful for teaching, rebuking, correcting and training in righteousness."*

These quotations and thousands of years of oral history provide the basis for inerrancy and the literal interpretation of the Bible. These verses make discussions with literal believers very difficult because it can lead to them patting their Bibles and saying, "You can argue with me, but you can't argue with God."

Inerrancy of the Bible means it is infallible, truthful and totally free of any errors. It means that all statements are historically, geographically and scientifically accurate.

But is inerrancy that important in the context of faith, belief in God, and being a Christian?

Can you still be a Christian if you don't believe in the infallibility or inspiration of the Bible? It may keep you from becoming a Baptist, Catholic, Lutheran or part of any particular denominational family, but you can still worship Jesus and God. You can still be a Christian.

Without the burden of following the teachings of a Christian denomination or sect, the idea of errors and inconsistencies become less bothersome. The fact that the authors had a story to tell about a Jesus that changed their lives is inspiring by itself.

In my own journey of faith it was important for me to answer a series of questions.

Why did early believers risk their lives to tell their story? What motivated them? What did Jesus actually say and do? And, most troubling, will my research draw me closer to God or drive me further away?

Growing up, my nearly constant exposure to the Bible combined with a very inquisitive nature often left me with questions. Unfortunately my minister brushed them away by saying I was not able to understand all the hidden meanings in the Bible. Besides, those biblical discrepancies were simply "small pieces of a very large puzzle." Apparently I was not to question, but to simply "believe."

I have always believed in God, however I do not believe in what early biblical writers told us about the Earth, universe or other non-scientific theories such as God making the sun stand still. These were the writings of those who loved God while attempting to explain complicated questions with limited knowledge.

Very early in my research it became troublesome that there were no surviving original texts of the Bible, including the four Gospels, telling the story of Jesus. There are only handwritten copies of copies of unknown origin. Even the stone tablets containing the Ten Commandments and the Arc of the Covenant—an elaborate box created by God to protect these precious tablets—have disappeared.

In addition, the books God is said to have personally dictated describing the life and teachings of his son Jesus, are also missing. The earliest surviving fragments of the original Gospels are copies of previous copies written from about 60–150 years after the birth of Christ.

In order to believe every word was directly inspired, we have to believe that each person who copied the text by hand was also inspired by God during their writing. This list of inspired writers would have to number in the hundreds.

Do you ever wonder why God, who is all-powerful and the creator of all things, did not preserve these important documents? Does this raise some suspicion? Why did God entrust these priceless documents to individuals who were so careless?

While reading the book of Mark a disturbing phrase caught my eye. In chapter 10 the Pharisees are testing Christ and ask if it is lawful for a man to divorce his wife. In verses 5–9 Christ changes Mosaic Law, which allowed a man to simply write a certificate of divorce and publicly proclaim his declaration, when he said, *"Therefore what God has joined together, let man not separate."* However it is his reasoning that caught my attention. In verse 5 Christ declares, *"It was because your hearts were hard that Moses wrote you this law."*

Jesus did not say, "God gave you this law," or "God wrote this law," or even the common phrase "it is written." What Jesus appears to be saying is that Moses wrote the laws for that given time and for a particular people. Those people had hardened hearts. Now Jesus seems to be indicating that because you are wiser and kinder there are new rules. If God makes no mistakes then we must conclude that someone wrote this down incorrectly.

This doubt in the inerrancy or inspiration of the Bible did not change my faith in God. In fact, it had the opposite effect. It has made me determined to learn where the books of the Bible originated, who wrote them, and what influenced the writing. In this way it allows me to better understand God and the teachings of Christ. By knowing more about the audience to whom Scripture was written, it provides me with a better understanding of the message of Christ.

All writers have a target audience for their writings and the writers of Scripture were no different. It is the responsible reader's task to discern the author's perspective to fully grasp the meaning of the work. Armed with this information we are able to place the information provided into its proper perspective. There are hundreds of Christian denominations who arrive at significantly different conclusions after studying an identical biblical passage. I have sat through hundreds of well-structured sermons thinking to myself that what I was hearing was a little "off message" for my own life. Have you ever felt somewhat disoriented after hearing a sermon?

As noted earlier, my formative years were inundated with the teachings of a conservative Baptist church. Our church was the focal point of my family life while growing up.

To this day the core of my faith has not changed. I believe Christ was sent to Earth by God to bring us a message of love and personal fulfillment. His actions and words give us a living example on how to live each moment of our lives to have the most fulfilling life imaginable, and that Jesus died on the cross and arose from the dead.

Like many, my beliefs are continually evolving. Unlike many organized religions, my beliefs are not orthodox. Early on I learned that the word orthodox has a much different meaning than what many think. The literal interpretation from Greek is "orthos: which translated is "right" and "doxa" which translates as "opinion." My journey is not the right opinion; it is simply my opinion, today. As my journey continues I trust God will keep surprising me at every turn in my life and keep providing a better understanding of my faith.

For those who would like to join in this journey to discover the mysteries of the Bible there are some wonderful resources. One that I've found helpful is *Jesus, Interrupted*, by biblical scholar Bart D. Ehrman. It is a well-researched and documented book in a very readable and factual format. His writing mirrors many of my beliefs on the origins of the Bible.

Any discussion regarding the inerrancy of the Bible must begin with the discovery of who actually wrote the Bible. While each book has a title, and most have been attributed to a specific author, research indicates that we really don't know who wrote most of the books.

Trying to determine authorship of the Old Testament is very difficult. The explanation that makes the most sense involves the concept called polyauthorism. The Old Testament contains 39 books and the best guess is that the surviving copies of those books were penned by dozens of authors over at least 600 years. Prior to these books being written down, the Old Testament was part of an oral tradition involving stories passed from generation to generation. As is the case with oral histories, words are changed and stories are exaggerated. This is human nature. It is very difficult to remember every detail when sharing stories with others.

There are literally hundreds of inconsistencies and contradictions in the Bible that are documented in numerous well-researched books by well-credentialed scholars. It is not my intent to pick through the Bible for errors. I will only mention a few obvious errors or contradictions that many Christians overlook.

Some biblical inconsistencies are hard to find, especially in the first reading. Growing up, my family read the Bible front to back for devotions. For those unfamiliar with the tradition of reading devotions, in our family it meant one person was selected, following each meal, to read a biblical passage out loud. Those gathered would listen and then comment on the reading. Reading devotions was a way to keep the Bible front and center in the life of our family.

One troubling aspect of the Gospels occurred to me during one of these readings. If God moved the hands of these authors to write the true and accurate story of Jesus' life here on Earth, why did he need to repeat the message four different times? It wasn't one story with multiple chapters, it was four people telling the same story in a different sequence, from four different perspectives. If God wrote these books, it seemed to me there would only be one perspective, not four. After all, if they were from the hand of God why are there four versions?

Biblical scholars read the Bible in a very different way than they would a traditional book. Unlike the method my parents used, reading from front to back, scholars use a method described very eloquently by Bart D. Ehrman in his book *Jesus, Interrupted*, called the historical-critical method. This method asks the reader to read the books of the Bible horizontally, comparing the texts. The method is especially useful when reading the New Testament, where all of the books were written during a seventy-year period. The four Gospels were all written about the events surrounding the life and crucifixion of Jesus. It is easy to compare a version of the birth of Jesus in Matthew with a similar version in Luke. Many of the parables, reporting healings and discussions, were present in two or three of the Gospels. My King James Version of the Bible actually references similar passages in the other books. When read in this manner, even minor contradictions become more evident.

In contrast, those raised in my parent's faith tradition read the Bible in a harmonizing fashion. We looked for harmony rather than conflict. My pastor was fond of saying that the books of the Bible were woven together like the fingers on a glove. This method of reading the Bible kept us from seeing and, therefore, discussing discrepancies. I was taught that Moses wrote the Pentateuch (the first five books of the Bible), Matthew (the disciple of Jesus) wrote the book of Matthew, Mark wrote the book of Mark, and that Paul of Tarsus wrote twelve books of the New Testament. We were also taught that God used these humans to create this one book. God was the one single author. It never occurred to me, at that young age, that the Bible was a collection of sixty-six short stories.

Now, as I compare these contradictions, what amazes me more than the actual discrepancies is the logic many in the church use to diminish the difference. A historian, when faced with two different versions of the same story, is forced to believe that either one account is accurate while the other is a fabrication, or that both are incorrect. The traditional Christian church takes a completely different approach. When faced with two different versions of the same story they combine parts of the two versions and create an entirely different story, a third version.

A great example is the story of the birth of Christ. Two of the four Gospels, Matthew and Luke, tell the story of Christ's birth but are surprisingly contradictory. I say surprisingly, since the church has so successfully woven the two accounts together, that every year we tell the story as one. Matthew states that Mary was *"pledged to be married to Joseph, but before they came together, she was found to be with child through the Holy Spirit. Because Joseph her husband was a righteous man and did not want to expose her to public disgrace, he had in mind to divorce her quietly."*

That is certainly an interesting choice of wording, to divorce her before their marriage. More importantly, an angel told Joseph that he should not be afraid to marry her as the child was conceived from the Holy Spirit. Joseph woke up and took her home as his wife, where she gave birth in their home in Bethlehem.

Do you notice anything missing from the story we all tell at Christmas? Where is the travel to Bethlehem by donkey to pay taxes, the swaddling clothes, the guiding star, the baby Jesus lying in the manger? They are not here, instead they are found in Luke. In Luke's version of this same story, the angel appears to Mary, not Joseph, and she apparently convinces Joseph of the miraculous event.

Luke states that Joseph and Mary lived in Nazareth and were forced to go to Bethlehem to pay taxes assessed by Caesar Augustus. This is an interesting journey as detailed by Bart Ehrman. Historians have very good records of the reign of Caesar Augustus, and there is no mention of this mandated tax in any of the documents. More incredibly Ehrman documents: "Joseph returns to Bethlehem because his ancestor, David, was born there. But David lived a thousand years before Joseph. Are we to imagine that everyone in the Roman Empire was required to return to the homes of their ancestors from a thousand years ago?"

Where would you go if ordered to pay taxes in the city where your forefathers lived one thousand years ago? Would you even know which country to visit?

As incredible as this seems, the church has adopted this part of the story, and we all accept it as true, even though it is contradicted in the Matthew version.

Luke also reported that the baby Jesus was born in a manger, with an angel informing the shepherds living in the fields nearby that a Savior had been born to you and they could *"find a baby wrapped in cloths and lying in a manger."* No wise men, no guiding star.

The same story in Matthew contained no shepherds but he did provide the wise men, and the guiding star that shone over the house where the baby Jesus was born. We have all seen stars in the sky, including the brightest star in our sky, the sun. If I directed you to find the house directly below the sun, where would you go? I don't know either, but I accepted this story for years.

Matthew also provided the story of King Herod and his orders to kill all the boys in Bethlehem who were under the age of two years. Joseph was warned by an angel of this danger, and he, Mary, and the baby left immediately to live in Egypt, until the death of Herod.

Luke's version had the family staying in Bethlehem where he was circumcised and named Jesus. When the time of purification was complete (this is a time that the mother must be cleansed after the staining of childbirth), according to Mosaic Law, they took him to Jerusalem to present him to the Lord. No travel to Egypt, no threat from Herod.

Many Christians are unaware of these discrepancies. Have you always believed that Mary and Joseph traveled to Bethlehem by donkey, that Jesus was born in a manger, and they were visited by wise men and shepherds? This is the third version of the events, created by the oral tradition of the church, which was not actually found in any of the books of the Bible. Oral teachings can provide a very powerful message even if the truth is speculative.

Another glaring discrepancy involves the different versions of creation found in Genesis chapters 1 and 2. Many are not aware there are actually two creation stories in the Bible. Chapter 2 tells another chronology of the creation story where man was created before the trees, Genesis 2:5 states: *"and no shrub of the field had yet appeared on the Earth and no plant of the field had yet sprung up."* Next in verse 7: *"the lord God formed the man from the dust of the ground"* Only in verse 9 did God make *"all kinds of trees grow out of the ground."*

In contrast, Genesis chapter 2 states man and woman are created together on the sixth day. It goes on to say man was created first, then the trees and rivers, then woman, then the beasts of the fields.

Are these discrepancies important? Not to me personally. However, for those who believe the Bible is inerrant it is difficult to balance these two versions. If chapter 1 is correct, then chapter 2 is incorrect—how do you explain the differences?

Growing up I loved the story of Moses and the Israelites escaping and surviving in the desert on the way to the Promised Land. The movie, *The Ten Commandments*, with Charlton Heston depicting Moses was a powerful story that I enjoy to this day.

While the movie is effective at harmonizing the events, the written account contains numerous contradictions. For example, we are told in Exodus 33:11: *"The Lord would speak to Moses face to face, as a man speaks with his friend."*

Shortly later in verse 20, God warns Moses: *"You cannot see my face, for no one may see me and live."*

Judges 1:1 establishes that Joshua is dead. However, in the very next chapter, Judges 2:6, Joshua dismisses an assembly of Israelites. There are several examples of rising from the dead in the Bible, but Joshua was not one of them.

These contradictions and omissions are found throughout the Bible, including another very obvious conflict with the outline of the life of Paul in the book of Acts with Paul's own words from his letters. What is important to Christians who are not literalists is that there was an amazing event that inspired numerous men to risk their lives to preserve this wonderful story. I believe that it is important to understand the motivations of the writers to truly understand the writings.

James L. Kugel, author of *How to Read the Bible* and a retired Starr professor of Hebrew Literature at Harvard University, states, "It is essential to be familiar with the teaching of the ancient interpreters of the Bible in order to fully appreciate the Bible." When reading the Bible, each book must be taken in the context of the author who wrote it, what they were teaching at that time, and to whom they were speaking.

Many prominent scholars, including those involved with the Jesus Seminar, believe that, with the exception of the seven books attributed to Paul (1 Thess, Gal, Phil, Phlm, I Cor, 2 Cor, and Rom), none of the books in the New Testament were written by the stated authors. In the Roman world documents were preserved by professional scribes who copied them one at a time, by hand. These scribes often made mistakes or, at times, edited the books to their liking. To date, we have not found one of the original books of the Bible written in the first century; most copies were penned in the middle of the second century, nearly 100 years after the original writing, and 150 years after the death of Jesus. Scholars estimate that the remaining twenty books may have had up to 117 authors written over a period of approximately seventy years.

When talking about the Bible, scholar Richard Elliot Friedman states that the Bible is: "the product of a community... the offspring of a continuing, developing culture."

It becomes very obvious that the authors of the various books compiled in the Bible had no idea they were writing one part of a continuing story. Instead they believed their writing stood alone. Paul, the most prolific writer in the New Testament, is credited with writing at least seven of the twenty-seven books. Some give him credit for writing an additional six books. All of Paul's books were actually letters written to churches that he had helped establish such as the "Letter to the Thessalonians" later shortened to "Thessalonians." It seems obvious that he was not intending to write a book in the Bible, but rather to simply convey a guiding message to the church members.

Some people are convinced that those who do not believe in the inerrancy of the Bible cannot be Christian. For myself, I believe I receive even more from the Bible after understanding what motivated these authors while attempting to discern the real message they were trying to convey. I find great comfort in reading the stories of Christ and his life on Earth along with his teaching through the use of parables.

While belief in the inerrancy may be required to be a member of some churches, I don't feel it is mandatory for being a Christian. In fact, it is my belief that it is easier to be a Christian when one questions the Bible. When asked which phrases are true and which are not, I feel the answer was best expressed by Tom Harpur in *The Pagan Christ* when he said: "Things are not true simply because they are collected in books such as the Bible. They are true because they ring with the full authenticity of the anvil of our souls."

2

A Closer Look at the Books of the Bible

Few Christians take the time to read the Gospels of the Bible critically. Fewer yet ask these simple questions: Where did we get the books of the Bible? Are there master copies of the four Gospels? Did God entrust these books to someone like he did with Moses and the tablets containing the Ten Commandments?

To gain a better understanding of the Gospels, it is helpful to introduce the authors.

The earliest surviving written account of Jesus' life was written thirty-five to sixty-five years after his death when the Gospel of Mark was written. Small fragments still survive, however it wasn't until another hundred years passed that a copy was transcribed which still survives today. What happened in the intervening years can be seen as miraculous.

Jesus, arguably the most influential person ever to walk the Earth, was not mentioned in any surviving record of the Greeks or Romans or any other pagan sources until the year 112 CE. Even though the Gospels report numerous clashes between Jesus and the Romans, the extensive written records of the Romans never mention him. Not until nearly eighty years after his death do we find a small reference regarding a civil disturbance involving a group of people calling themselves Christians. That doesn't mean that the conflicts didn't occur, however if they did occur they were likely to be such minor skirmishes they did not warrant inclusion in the written record. These may be explained away as simple inconveniences to the ruling Romans, however they were significant events to the early Christians. Another possibility is that they never occurred. Beyond the Bible there are no other written records that support the historical accounts in the Gospels.

Yet in the intervening years something miraculous was happening. For some reason, the actions of this carpenter from a small village created a religion that rocked the world.

Immediately after his death his followers, somewhere between fifteen and twenty men and women, left their jobs and families and began an unprecedented missionary effort across the Mediterranean.

By the end of the first century these twenty had told, and retold, the miraculous story of the risen Christ. As a result, Christianity spread throughout Judea, Samaria, Galilee, Syria, into Cilicia, throughout what is now Turkey, Greece, all the way to Rome and possibly as far as Spain, Egypt, and North Africa. This is truly an amazing effort for a group with no funding, no mass transit, no form of modern communication, no written text to guide them, and no official doctrine.

Imagine someone traveling on foot to your village and asking for a moment of your time. Even though he is a complete stranger, it is obvious his story is one he is bursting to share. With intrigue you listen, in spite of his rather crude presentation. With conviction the visitor speaks about a life-changing event he has witnessed. You become a believer, and return home to share his incredible story with your family and friends. Because you share the message in such a convincing manner they too are converted, and begin to tell the wondrous story of Jesus to others.

Have you ever experienced a similar conversion from a stranger? I have heard some fabulous storytellers, but I have never been moved to leave the comfort of my home and become a traveling evangelist.

In the Gospels there are no indications that the disciples were eloquent or convincing speakers. This leaves me with the conclusion that it was the substance of the story they told, their recollections of Jesus and the resurrection of Christ, that caused the conversion of so many people, over such a large area, in such a short time.

I believe that something unworldly must have accompanied this man Jesus to cause such an amazing number of conversions under such difficult circumstances.

Another important conclusion one can make concerns the rules of oral tradition. As anyone who has played the game of "telephone" knows, the message often gets mixed with each retelling. Telephone is the game where you whisper a story from one person to the next until you arrive at the end of the line. Without exception, when the last person shares the story with the rest of the group, the message is considerably different from the original. This principle is magnified when people travel from village to village and across cultural lines over many decades. With each telling of the story it can become better or worse and richer or shallower, depending on the speaker. Emphasis undoubtedly changes, as do the words. The perspective of a former sun worshiper is different than that of a Jew and the message is slightly altered with each telling and each audience.

I have a great friend who is a wonderful storyteller. He will capture a room with stories of events that happened to the two of us. Each time he retells a story, it becomes better, with greater details and typically with the introduction of new "facts." He is so compelling that I sometimes find it hard to remember the actual event.

This chain of stories originally told by the disciples went on for over thirty-five years. In a short time great numbers of people were converted even though the recipients had never met Jesus. In fact, many didn't know anyone who knew Christ.

The most prolific missionary and the founder of modern Christianity was Paul of Tarsus, or St. Paul as he is referred to in the Catholic Church. Paul authored at least seven of the twenty-seven books of the New Testament. Even though Paul began teaching a few years after the death of Christ, he never met Jesus in person. His conversion was the result of a dramatic light from heaven where he met

Jesus in a vision, unseen by the men that accompanied him. Paul's writings indicate that this was his only contact with Jesus.

Paul writes primarily about what he learned from this vision, his personal beliefs, and the risen Christ. His writings indicate that he probably did not have access to the Gospels or their sources during his travels.

Most Christian churches still teach the New Testament as if it consists of first-hand accounts of the life of Jesus. Unfortunately, none of the books of the Bible were written by people who actually knew or even met Jesus, let alone witnessed the events attributed to him. With such incredible events happening before their eyes, the logical question that arises is: "Why didn't at least one of the disciples take the time to write things down?" There are probably many reasons for this, but two come to mind.

From reading the Gospels, it is clear that the disciples were manual laborers from a very poor area in Galilee. The possible exception may be the disciple Matthew, who is reported to be a tax collector. As there are many levels of people collecting taxes from the assessor to the man knocking on your door to take your money, we are not certain of his education. It is estimated that fewer than ten percent of the people in Galilee during that time were literate. It would be rare for a fisherman to know how to read. Acts 4:13 tells us that they were illiterate, *"when they saw the courage of Peter and John and realized that they were unschooled, ordinary men, they were astonished."*

Jesus and all of his disciples, including Matthew, spoke Aramaic. The writers of the Gospels were well-educated and experienced writers that wrote in Greek. This precludes Matthew from being the author of the book that bears his name.

According to the Gospels, the disciples were not raised with Jesus and they chose to drop everything to follow him at their first meeting. They didn't have any idea who he was, but his words and commanding presence compelled them to follow him. In their discussions with Christ, it is clear that they do not comprehend who he is through most of their travels and time together. They have hunches and suspicions, but there were other great apocalyptic prophets in that time, most notably John the Baptist, who commanded a significant following.

It is my belief that it was only after the resurrection that the disciples truly understood and believed that Christ was the Son of God. Only after he was gone, did they realize what they had witnessed. Had any of the disciples been able to write as events were unfolding they would have captured the events more accurately, and there would have been no need for four separate versions, or books.

Keeping in mind that none of the original writings survived, when scholars examine the Gospels it becomes clear that Mark was the first to be written and that Matthew and Luke used his text as a basis for their own writings. It is also generally accepted that an earlier book of the teachings of Christ was available and circulating at that time. Researchers have called this lost book Quelle, the German word for "source." In their scholastic discussions, they shorten this to "Q" which is believed to be a source of common sayings attributed to Jesus found in both Matthew and Luke, however these sayings were not found in Mark.

Of the four original attempts to record the life of Jesus, only tiny fragments of Mark survived. Although no copies of the other three original documents have been found, by examining the Gospels, many scholars believe that the surviving three Gospels used these four sources to create their books. This is referred to as the Four-Source theory, which to me makes the most sense.

The original Mark and Q are the earliest independent sources. It is believed that the book of Matthew that has survived used another oral or written source which has been called the book of "M." The surviving book of Luke also had a prior source unique to his writing that is designated the book of "L." Therefore, prior to Matthew and Luke there were at least four sources we know of that they used to complete their writings, Mark, Q, M, and L. From these four original sources, only three Gospels survived and are referred to as the Synoptic Gospels.

Somewhere between thirty and sixty years after the crucifixion, Mark, Q, M, and L put many of the stories of Jesus and the parables he told into written form. This made the telling of the stories easier and more uniform.

When Matthew began writing his book, he had access to original source M, Mark and the sayings from Q. When Luke wrote his book, he had access to Mark, Q, as well as an independent source, L.

To support the scholastic opinion that Mark was written first and was used by Matthew and Luke, it is helpful to examine the comparison of these books provided by the authors of *The Five Gospels*.

"Matthew reproduces about 90 percent of Mark, Luke about 50 percent. They often reproduce Mark in the same order. When they disagree, either Matthew or Luke supports the sequence in Mark. Matthew and Mark often agree against Luke, and Luke and Mark often agree against Matthew, but Matthew and Luke only rarely agree against Mark."

The fourth book, the book of John, is significantly different than the first three and appears to come from a fifth source, the Gospel of Signs. Most of this book consists of very long stories and sermons attributed to Jesus. One of them, found in books 13–16, requires nearly four chapters to tell. Because of the long narratives quoted in John, this may not be an accurate reflection of what Jesus taught.

I believe that it is important to repeat that the authors of the Gospels were not writing a chapter to be combined with others to form a single book, the Bible. Each additional version was not an attempt to continue the story, but instead, to correct a perceived error. This was not a consolidated effort to publish one book to guide our lives. Their entire goal is to create a single report that reflects the life of Jesus, as they perceived it. They did not even bother to put a name on the story. The titles, such as the book of Mark, were added later by the church.

Some, like the author of Matthew, believed this was not even a new religion, but a continuation of Judaism, and that the life of Jesus was a fulfillment of the prophecies found in the Torah. This led Matthew to repeatedly refer to the *"fulfillment of the prophecies"* and add words to the text like *"as is written"* even when reporting a direct quotation from Jesus.

As these four original versions of the history and teachings of Jesus were being written and circulated, other competing stories were also being circulated orally. Many of these slightly different versions eventually were made into written transcripts. In fact, we have fragments or copies of over forty-four different Gospels, in addition to those found in the Christian Bible, that were circulating at this time.

When the content of the Christian Bible was being standardized, creating the "canon of scripture," the remainder of these books were omitted and discredited by the church. At the time, there was significant disagreement as to which of these books were the authoritative scripture; a disagreement that continues to this day. The Roman Catholic canon is different from the Protestant canon, which is different from the Orthodox canon. Even Martin Luther attempted to remove the books of Hebrews, James, Jude, and Revelation from what became the Lutheran Bible because he thought God did not authorize them. He was unsuccessful, however; these books were placed in the back of the German-language Lutheran Bible.

Books that claim to be authored by Judas, Mary Magdalene, and Thomas are currently causing significant discussion in the Christian community and could be added by some denominations in the future.

An examination of the beginning of each of the four Gospels helps us to recognize the perspective of the author. Matthew and Luke are the only two that tell the story of the virgin birth. It appears that this was added from the original texts, as the earliest existing writings—those of Paul and Mark—do not mention the virgin birth. In fact, Paul indicates that Jesus was born of a normal birth.

Galatians 4:4 *"But when the time had fully come, God sent his son, born of a woman, born under the law, to redeem under the law, that we might receive the full rights of sons."*

At the time of the writing of Matthew and Luke, the Mediterranean region was filled with religions and mythologies of gods that were born of virgins. It was almost a pre-requisite for deity. In Greek mythology both Perseus and Dionysius were born of virgins. Persian god Mithra was conceived when God entered a virgin in the form of light. The Phoenician god Adonis was born of the virgin Myrrh. It is a strong possibility that the idea of a virgin birth was added to the accounts of Mark to provide legitimacy to Jesus.

The story of the virgin birth is also puzzling given Mary's response to the actions of Jesus. In the second chapter of Luke, Mary and Joseph traveled for a day without realizing that the twelve-year-old Jesus had remained in the temple in Jerusalem. He was teaching and the parents were "astonished." In the third chapter of Mark, after finding the disciples, he was teaching in a home so filled with listeners that they were unable to eat.

Mark 3:21 *"When his family heard about this, they went to take charge of him, for they said, 'He is out of his mind.'"*

If Mary knew that God was the father of her child, why would she be surprised that he would be teaching? Would she consider his radical teachings as insane?

Matthew taught that the virgin birth was actually fulfillment of the prophesies found in Isaiah 7:14 which makes reference to the prophesy that a baby would be born of a virgin. Some scholars claim that the original Hebrew word used did not indicate a virgin but rather a young woman. While I do not know if this is true, it is clear that the reference to fulfilling the scriptures would assist Matthew and Luke in making their case that this was not a new religion and instead a continuation of Judaism.

I am convinced that Jesus was the embodiment of God on Earth and that his resurrection provided final proof to his disciples that what they had witnessed was the greatest event in the history of the Earth.

It is unfortunate that we do not have any surviving first-hand accounts from the men and women who accompanied Jesus on his journeys. Instead, by using simple and logical rules of oral tradition, we can discern part of Jesus' original message and perhaps some of his actual words.

Scholars provide a few valuable and logical rules to assist in our search to discover the message of Jesus. In attempting to determine what he actually said, there are common sense rules, used by biblical scholars that need to be applied to words attributed to Jesus.

First, it is easier to remember and correctly repeat a short phrase when memorable and repeated often. Long sermons and speeches, such as those attributed to Jesus in the book of John, would be nearly impossible to repeat verbatim over decades of oral storytelling. How could anyone be expected to remember something so long, especially word for word? However, for example, the "I am" verses from John, very easily meet this criteria. *"I am the light of the world"* is both short and provocative. One could see how someone could remember it, and repeat it accurately, years into the future.

Think about your own experiences. Can you remember the last sermon or speech that really inspired you? Or how about a transforming political or motivational talk. What specifically do you remember? Could you quote the entire speech, verbatim? Few could. In fact, it is unlikely that anyone could recite a single paragraph word-for-word. Many can remember the general outline of a presentation or recall a simple one-sentence phrase. One might leave an event with a wonderful feeling or be able to recall a story using one's own words and phrases while communicating only the general message.

Now, think back ten years to a speech or sermon that was transformational. What do you remember about it? You may recall a particular phrase or be able to evoke a feeling from listening to it. But who could recount it word-for-word ten years later?

One hears of born-again Christians remembering the experience of accepting Jesus as their Lord and Savior. However if asked to remember the entirety of the words of the sermon that moved them they would undoubtedly only remember a sentence or phrase but not the entire message.

Looking back at some of the great orations in history, generally, people only remember a short phrase. For example, Patrick Henry proclaimed: "Is life so dear, or peace so sweet, as to be purchased at the price of chains and slavery? Forbid it, Almighty God! I know not what course others may take; but as for me, give me liberty, or give me death!"

Even though the first sentence is critical to understanding the enormous threat he was facing, most only remember the last seven words.

Martin Luther King's speech from the Lincoln Memorial was truly inspiring when he proclaimed that he had a dream of a country that was free of prejudice and hatred. It was a speech that changed the nation. However, most only recall the phrases "I have a dream" and "free at last."

President John Kennedy gave a stirring inaugural address in 1961 when he declared: "Finally, whether you are citizens of America or citizens of the world, ask of us the same high standards of strength and sacrifice which we ask of you. With a good conscience our only sure reward, with history the final judge of our deeds, let us go forth to lead the land we love, asking His blessing and His help, but knowing that here on earth God's work must truly be our own."

A great ending to a wonderful speech, but the only exact memory that lingers was the phrase: "And so, my fellow Americans: ask not what your country can do for you—ask what you can do for your country."

As you can see, even with the advantages of the printing press, a recorded radio transmission and the imagery of television, exact memories are limited. One cannot remember entire speeches or repeat, word-for-word, a story for minutes, let alone decades, without that story changing.

Great orators know that they must repeat something at least three times during the speech for the audience to remember, or that they must use a phrase that is extremely unique or contrary to common thought. Martin Luther King and John F. Kennedy were good examples. They were aware people would not remember an entire speech.

This is magnified when stories are handed from generation to generation. It would be virtually impossible that sermons attributed to Jesus would survive intact, through the decades of retelling, before being written down.

Secondly, great orators often use parables or stories to make a point. Many believe Jesus used this method to provoke his audience. While it is difficult to imagine these stories are repeated verbatim, Jesus probably used them to teach those who gathered. The book of Q is believed to be a series of aphorisms and parables. John clearly did not use Q as a source as he is the only Gospel writer that does not show Jesus teaching in parables.

The parables attributed to Jesus are probably not recorded word-for-word in the Scripture, but they are most likely stories very similar to parables used by Jesus.

Third, the sayings and parables that were most likely remembered were those that surprised and shocked Jesus' audiences. In many instances, they were teachings that were contrary to the prevailing teachings from the Torah. A Jew who heard Jesus say *"he who is without sin should cast the first stone"* would remember it because that goes contrary to the teachings of the synagogue that all adulterers should be stoned to death.

Another complication is that of translation. The native language of Jesus and his disciples was Aramaic. The Gospels also report that he taught in the temple, therefore, it would not be a stretch to say that Jesus may also have knowledge of Hebrew. However, the only written records of the words attributed to Jesus that have been preserved were written in Greek. Further complicating this is that the Bible is translated into every written language and certain words and phrases can change meaning and inferences during translation.

I remember clearly the concerned and shocked look on my Brazilian exchange student's face the first time I told him that I would "pick him up" after school. As he envisioned me placing him on my shoulders, I quickly explained that I simply meant to communicate that I was willing to transport him home, in our car. My friend Debbie, a southern belle, is fond of saying she is "fixin' to go" somewhere. She is clearly not referring to repairing anything, as the language would indicate.

All speech is filled with phrases and words that do not completely explain the circumstances and intent of the author to someone from another culture or language. The issue of differences in translation is even evident when comparing different translations of the Bible such as the older King James Version (KJV) and more recent New International Version (NIV). I remember my pastor, when arguing against adoption of the NIV saying, "If thee and thou were good enough for Jesus, they are good enough for me." This from a man who was most certainly taught during seminary that

Jesus spoke Aramaic and the original biblical writings were in Greek. Jesus did not speak English so he certainly would not have used the words "thee" or "thou."

Like most Christians, I spent years trying to discern the true message of this inerrant text, the Bible. I was asking "what?" when I should have been asking "who?" Who wrote these books that we treasure as "holy"? The things I have written in this chapter are not revelations; your minister knows, or should know, as this is typically part of seminary studies.

The Old Testament was written hundreds of years after the reported events, by an unknown group of writers attempting to document the incredible journey of the Jewish People and glorifying a God of their ancestors. It is not science, it is not accurate history, and it establishes rules that most Christians, and the majority of Jewish sects, no longer follow.

The Gospels were written by individuals that did not speak the same language as Jesus, never met Jesus, and used copies of books that were written decades after the death of Jesus. The earliest surviving copies of our existing books of the Gospels were not written until 150 years after Jesus died. The quotations attributed to Jesus were the "best recollections" of what Jesus was reported to have said, interpreted by devout followers of Christ.

Paul, who never met Jesus, recorded a series of writings that he used to coordinate new members and codify a message about a risen Christ. He did this using his God-given logic and his best understanding of the message of Jesus.

Given this knowledge, it is our responsibility to attempt to discern the true message of Christ, which allows us to find the kingdom of God within us.

3

The People Who Wrote the Bible

In order to truly understand the message from the Bible, it is critical to know who wrote it. There are a multitude of scholars that have a deep understanding of this topic. Authors like Bart D. Ehrman, Gary Willis, John Shelby Spong, James L. Kugel and the scholars of the Jesus Seminar are excellent sources for this complex topic. The contents of this chapter summarize some of their findings along with my own experiences.

I was taught that Moses was the primary author of the Old Testament since he wrote arguably the most important collection of books called the Pentateuch. The Pentateuch consists of the first five books of the Bible (Genesis, Exodus, Leviticus, Numbers, and Deuteronomy). The laws of the Israelites, that were given to Moses, are referred to as Mosaic Laws and are found primarily in these five books as is the creation story, the story of the exodus from Egypt, the tower of Bable, Noah's Ark, and numerous core stories and traditions that Christians find familiar.

There are no passages in any of these books that make a claim of Moses being the author. Most scholars now believe he was not the author. Evidence strongly indicates that several anonymous authors probably wrote these books.

The book of Psalms, a collection of songs and poetry, was originally attributed to Kings David and Solomon. Scholars now attribute the authorship to multiple unknown writers several hundred years after the death of these two kings.

Another good example of this poly-authorism is the book of Isaiah. It is commonly accepted by biblical scholars that it was written by three different authors. The first thirty-nine chapters were most likely written around the eighth century BCE, chapters forty to fifty-five were written two hundred years later in the sixth century BCE, and the final ten chapters were added even later.

The book of Isaiah, specifically the second writer that penned verses forty to fifty-five, is critical for the Christian community because it introduces the concept of atonement; that Christ was sent by God to suffer and die for the sins of humankind. Knowing when this important book was written is critical to understanding the perspective of the author as well as the meaning of these verses.

Nearly every book in the Old Testament was written by unknown scribes, most likely taking the oral storytelling of each generation and writing it down to create a "history" of the Jewish faith and travels.

This change in authorship does not compromise the value of reading the Old Testament. It does, however, make the case for inerrancy much more difficult as God would now have to inspire everyone who originally told the story. Then, God would similarly have to inspire every person who passed the story along to future generations along with each scribe that originally composed the written text. After that God would have to inspire everyone who created a hand crafted copy of the previous text (prior to the invention of the printing press) and everyone who translated the text from the original language.

No doubt God could accomplish this series of events, but to do so is mind boggling. Wouldn't it have been easier to simply preserve a copy of the original text? Just like the stones of the Ten Commandments, none of the original Old Testament texts are preserved.

The Gospels

The first four books of the New Testament are typically referred to as the "Gospels." In the King James Version they are referred to as The Gospel according to St. Matthew, The Gospel of St. Mark, The Gospel According to St. Luke and The Gospel According to St. John.

When one reads a book titled The Gospel According to St. Matthew, and you know that Jesus had a disciple called Matthew, many people assume that these were the thoughts and writings of the disciple of that name.

In fact, the first surviving copies of the Gospels were not titled, but were assigned names by Irenaeus, the church father in the year 180, to separate the four gospels he selected from the many others that were circulating that he deemed heretical. Books like the book of Thomas, the book of Mary, the book of Judas, and the book of James were discarded in favor of the twenty-seven which were selected.

Whoever wrote the book of Matthew may well have been re-telling the story related to him by people that knew the disciple of the same name. However, the author is clearly writing in the third person when referring to Matthew. Matthew 9:9 states: *"As Jesus went on from there, he saw a man named Matthew sitting at the tax collector's booth. 'Follow me,' he told him and Matthew got up and followed him."*

Being objective, if you were writing about the most significant event in your life—the day Jesus saw and recruited you to be his disciple—would you write it in such a detached way? I would talk about Jesus speaking to "me," and recruiting "me." This author makes no such claim.

More importantly, it seems to me that attributing the disciple Matthew as the author diminishes the credibility of all of the previous text in the book including the beautiful collections referred to as the Beatitudes. Matthew does not meet Christ until chapter 9. Chapters 5 through 7 contain over 115 verses that are direct quotes from Jesus. In the red-letter edition of the NIV Bible, where all the quotes attributed to Christ are written in red, it is essentially six solid pages of red. How would Matthew know what Jesus said, if he hadn't met him yet?

The author of Mark was not a disciple, however we were taught that he was a follower of Peter. Church officials now claim that an ancient book written by Papias dating to approximately 120 CE, validates the claim that Mark was written by the interpreter of Peter. Papias also states that the book provides the recollections of Peter, of the words spoken by Jesus. He also states that the "words and deeds" of Jesus are accurate, however the sequence is not correct.

The author of Luke states unequivocally that he is attempting to hand down to Theophilus an account from the eyewitnesses who knew Jesus. It is known that Peter had a companion named Luke. Scholars believe that the writing in this book is nearly identical in form and substance with that found in the book of Acts which chronicles Peter's journeys and teachings. For these reasons scholars believe that the same author, whoever he was, wrote both of these books.

John was clearly one of the named disciples of Christ, but it is believed that he is not the author of the book of John. The disciple John was a fisherman and it is highly unlikely that he could read or write. It is reported in the book of Acts that John was "unlettered."

A better reference to the authorship is found in the last chapter of John. John 21:24 states: *"This is the disciple who testifies to these things and who wrote them down. We know that his testimony is true."* Clearly, the author is not claiming to be John the disciple, but rather claiming he is recording his message.

In summary, these four books are very different because they were written by people who didn't know Jesus, or most likely didn't even know people who knew Jesus. Clearly, the authors were from a different country than Jesus, spoke a different language, and were writing at least forty years after his death. The startling differences of the content and records of these four books is not an attempt at distortion, but most likely a result of the different perspective of each of the authors. We will discuss some of these differences in a little more detail.

Where Did Jesus Come From?

The two different accounts of the birth of the baby Jesus, in Matthew and Luke, is an interesting study in how we easily overlook contradictions and discrepancies. The Jesus story we repeat at Christmas reflects a unified beginning for Jesus in a manger in Bethlehem, being born of a virgin. The Gospels tell a significantly different story.

Of the four Gospels, only two recount the birth of Jesus. Mark begins with the story of John the Baptist who meets Jesus in the very first chapter. There is no mention of the virgin birth, no travel to Bethlehem, not even a Mary and Joseph. For the author of Mark, the first book written and used by Matthew and Luke, the most significant event that occurs in the development of Jesus is him being baptized. For Mark, the baptism was the event that changed Jesus to the Christ, not when he was born.

A humorous aside. When I was growing up, we thought his name was Jesus Christ. This was because the sermons we heard contained many references in this manner. As a result I assumed that Joseph and Mary Christ were his parents. Later I learned Christ is actually from the Greek word *Christos* which means "anointed." Any reference I make to when Jesus became Christ means after he was anointed and became either God or Godlike.

Matthew and Luke, while varying on how or where the virgin birth occurred, clearly believe that God impregnated Mary and she gave birth to Christ as a virgin. In these books, Jesus came into existence and was the Christ at conception, when God impregnated Mary, which increases the importance of the virgin birth.

John, unlike the other three, begins his book by stating that Jesus, the Word, was always in existence and always the Christ, by declaring in the first verse of the first chapter: *"In the beginning was the Word, and the Word was with God, and the Word was God. He was with God in the beginning."*

33

As I mentioned earlier, of the four books, John is significantly different than the Synoptic Gospels. John acknowledges that John the Baptist knew Jesus, but does not document the first significant event of the other three books, the baptism of Jesus and the temptation in the wilderness.

While the church has been extremely effective at weaving these four unique stories together, as we discussed regarding the story of the birth of Jesus, they are clearly four independent accounts and explanations for the presence of Christ here on Earth.

How did Jesus Teach?

Parables are stories that paint a word picture that creates a story or an image to teach a lesson. Many rabbis used parables at the time of Jesus. According to the Synoptic Gospels, Jesus also used this memorable tool in his sermons and everyday discussions. Many of these parables, such as the mustard seed, a camel fitting through an eye of a needle, the patch and the wine skins, and the Good Samaritan, are familiar to most Christians. Mark went so far as to claim that Jesus only taught the crowds using parables.

Mark 4:34 *"He did not say anything to them without using a parable."*

Many of the parables are repeated in all three Synoptic Gospels though often in different settings.

The book of John, using a different source, did not attribute a single parable to Jesus. John typically has Jesus preaching long sermons, many of which are detailed over several chapters.

Clearing of the Temple and the Last Supper

The three Synoptic Gospels all agree that when Jesus entered Jerusalem, he became upset that the temple was filled with money changers, and people selling doves and sheep. The famous outcry that they are making the house of God a den of thieves shows his anger as he overturns the tables and frees the animals of sacrifice. They also agree that this action, in addition to defying other Jewish customs, angered the chief priests, and ultimately leads to his death.

The book of John also describes Jesus clearing the temple, but in his account it occurs in the beginning of Jesus' ministry and is reported in the second chapter.

We are also very familiar with the depiction of the Last Supper by Leonardo da Vinci, and the story reported in the Synoptic Gospels. This is an important event that is celebrated either weekly or monthly in most Christian churches with the breaking of the bread (the body of Christ) and the drinking of the wine (the blood of Christ).

Again, John deviates from this important ritual. In chapter 13:4–5 John reports that following the evening meal, Jesus: *"… took off his outer clothing, and wrapped a towel around his waist. After that, he poured water into a basin and began to wash his disciples' feet, drying them with the towel that was wrapped around him."*

There is no discussion of the eating of the "body" and drinking the "blood of Christ." Instead, he explains to Peter the importance of the washing of feet when he states in verse 8: *"Unless I wash you, you have no part with me."*

For John, the most important event is the washing of the feet of the disciples. John then reports nearly seven full pages of direct quotations from Jesus with no mention of the Last Supper.

When Does Jesus Admit that He is the Christ?

The Gospels are not united on the very important topic of how Jesus viewed himself, or on when he admits that he was the Christ.

In Mark's account, when confronted by Peter that he is the Messiah, Jesus does not dispute Peter's declaration that he is the Christ. However Jesus does not claim to be the Son of Man or the Messiah until confronted by the high priest a second time when he declares in Mark 14:61–62: *"I am, and you will see the Son of*

Man sitting at the right hand of the Mighty One and coming on the clouds of heaven."

In Matthew and Luke, Jesus often refers to himself as the *"Son of Man"* and on several occasions immediately instructs the disciples that they should not tell anyone.

The book of John is very clear on who Jesus is and who he says he is and that he wants everyone to know. It contains some of the most well known verses including my favorite, John 3:16, and his "I am" sayings.

"I am the light of the world." (John 8:12)

"I am the bread of life." (John 6:35)

"I am the living bread that came down from heaven." (John 6:51)

"I am from him." (John 7:29)

"I am the good shepherd." (John 10:11)

"I am the resurrection and the life." (John 11:25)

Jesus spends a significant amount of time telling the disciples that he and God are the same.

"I and the father are one." (John 10:30)

Was Jesus secretive about being the Son of God? Did he brag about his authority in his speeches? We may never know as the Gospels do not provide a clear answer.

The Last Days of Jesus

Any attempt to determine exactly what happened at the end of Jesus' life becomes increasingly difficult as none of the authors claim to be present during many of the most significant events. Only the book of John makes any claim to being familiar with the disciples when it states in the next to last verse: *"This is the disciple who testifies to these things and who wrote them down. We know that his testimony is true."*

The author only claims that "his" testimony is true, not "my testimony."

While examining the stories of what Jesus said to Pilate during his interrogation, or what Jesus said while praying in the garden of Gethsemane, it becomes evident that the disciples were not present to witness these events. How could they possibly know what was said? Growing up, my pastor would tell me that God told them what to write which is consistent with the concept of the inspiration of the Word. As we have discussed, this argument loses its validity with the exposition of these serious discrepancies.

We have all heard the story of how Judas betrayed Jesus and later hanged himself. While all four books report the betrayal by Judas, only the book of Matthew reports that he was so filled with remorse that he returned the money and committed suicide.

With the recent discovery of the book of Judas, many scholars are re-examining the role of Judas in the Christ story. How could Judas be a villain in this story if Jesus needed to be betrayed to complete his mission? Without Judas, the crucifixion would not occur and the death of Jesus would have been delayed. Judas was an important part of this story and was doing what God had pre-destined. He was simply playing his part in this important drama.

John did not see the role of Judas as predetermined, but instead a villainous Jew worthy of eternal damnation.

John 19:11 *"Therefore the one who handed me over to you is guilty of a greater sin."*

A sign outside a local church recently proclaimed that "God had a plan for your life even before you were born." Was this the plan for Judas? Did Judas have any choice other than to betray Jesus? If God has preordained our every movement, then why was the betrayal by Judas reprehensible? He was performing God's will as an integral part of the fulfillment of Jesus' mission on Earth.

John reports that after he prayed, Jesus crossed the Kidron Valley where he was arrested in an olive grove.

Luke states that Jesus went to the Mount of Olives where he left the disciples to pray alone and was arrested following the prayer.

Matthew and Mark report that Jesus went to a place called Gethsemane where he left the disciples to pray. However, Mark reports that Jesus was not alone with the disciples at the time of his arrest. In chapter 14 of Mark, Jesus was seized by a crowd that accompanied Judas. Someone attempted to defend Jesus by cutting the ear off one of the men. Jesus intervened and verse 50 and 51 tells us: *"Then everyone deserted him and fled. A young man, wearing nothing but a linen garment, was following Jesus. When they seized him, he fled naked, leaving his garment behind."*

Since Mark was the first book written, and used by both Matthew and Luke, it is very interesting that both authors decided to omit this strange event. This verse has been quoted by some in the gay community to support the assertion that Jesus may have been gay. He was apparently still single at the age of thirty-three, when most people in that era married in their early teens, and he traveled primarily with men. This seems a stretch to me; however, it is a very unusual sentence to conclude Mark's account of this significant event.

The way Jesus interacted with Pilate was very enlightening. In Mark and Matthew, Jesus confuses Pilate and the chief priest with his unwillingness to speak. At the trial before Pilate, Jesus remains silent except for a single response to Pilate's question, *"Are you the king of the Jews?"* Jesus replied: *"Yes, it is as you say."*

Other than this sentence he remains silent and is seemingly willing to accept his pre-ordained fate. Luke agrees with this reply to Pilate, however he adds a separate confrontation with the church elders and a hearing before Herod.

In John, Jesus is far from quiet and meek. He challenges the high priest repeatedly as in chapter 18 verse 23: *"If I said something wrong, testify as to what is wrong. But if I spoke the truth, why did you strike me?"*

He is equally confrontational to Pilate:

John 18:34 *"Is that your idea, or did others talk to you about me?"*

John 18:36 *"My kingdom is not of this world. If it were, my servants would fight to prevent my arrest by the Jews. But now my kingdom is from another place."*

John 19:11 *"You would have no power over me if I were not given to you from above."*

Clearly, at least two different perspectives of Jesus are presented, not the cohesive story taught in our Sunday Schools. In reality, both seem to be created by the authors to reflect their perception of Jesus. None of the authors were present nor is there any report of Jesus reporting his activities during the trial.

The Crucifixion

The story of the crucifixion is, much like the story of Jesus' birth, not a single cohesive story, as has been taught, but rather a compilation of all four stories woven into one.

In Mark and Matthew, Jesus remains silent through all the mocking and punishment.

In Luke, as Jesus is being led to the cross, he once more speaks to the women who are mourning using a parable of barren women. All four books mention that two others were crucified with Jesus, one on each side, however Luke is the only version that includes a discussion with the criminals.

Mark and Matthew agree that his only words while on the cross are: Mark 15:34 *"My God, My God, why have you forsaken me?"*

Luke adds significantly to the report. Jesus proclaims the very familiar phrase in Luke 23:34 *"Father, forgive them, for they do not know what they are doing."*

In addition, Luke reports Jesus telling the repentant criminal that he will join Jesus in paradise that day. Luke also completely changes the final words of Jesus. He reports: Luke 23:46 *"Father, into your hands I commit my spirit."*

John offers a third version of the crucifixion. Near the cross, Jesus sees his mother and the disciple who he loved and declares:

John 19:25–27 *"Near the cross of Jesus stood his mother, his mother's sister, Mary the wife of Clopas, and Mary Magdalene. When Jesus saw his mother there, and the disciple whom he loved standing nearby, he said to his mother, 'Dear woman, here is your son' and to the disciple, 'Here is your mother.'"*

Various groups with a particular agenda interpret this phrase differently. Depending upon your perspective the "disciple whom he loved" could be his gay lover, Mary Magdalene, or simply the disciple Peter, who was Jesus' most trusted disciple.

John then reports his finals words as being; John 19:28 and 30 *"I am thirsty."* and *"It is finished."*

While these are relatively minor differences, the church molds these four stories into one cohesive story that is repeated every Easter. Nobody is able to answer the basic question, "which of these stories is correct?" However, the most pertinent question from my perspective is, "who was present to witness these events?"

Was Jesus submissive and accepting of his crucifixion or was he confrontational to the authority figures and Jews? The Bible teaches us that the disciples scattered and none of the Gospels report the presence of any of the male disciples throughout the trial and crucifixion process. Was anyone close enough to actually hear what Jesus said on the cross? It is possible that the women who John names were fairly close, however, the book attributed to Mary Magdalene was not part of the official Canon and is regarded as a forgery by the church. Without her testimony, we can never be certain.

Different Perspectives from Different Authors

In the book of Mark, the message of Jesus is focused on the impending arrival of the kingdom of God which will eliminate the pain and suffering people have endured. Jesus offers relief from this pain and suffering with a message that this suffering will end very soon.

Mark 9:1 *"I tell you the truth, some who are standing here will not taste death before they see the kingdom of God come with power."*

Mark 13:30 *"I tell you the truth, this generation will certainly not pass away until all these things have happened."*

When the original author of Mark wrote this book (around 60 CD), many in his audience were alive when Jesus taught of the second coming of Christ. His message was still valid as long as this generation lived.

In fact, both Mark and Luke agree that Jesus promised that the event would occur in their generation.

Luke 9:27 *"I tell you the truth, some who are standing here will not taste death before they see the kingdom of God."*

However as time passed, and the apocalyptic version of the kingdom of God had still not happened, this story became somewhat suspect. They either had to change the concept of the kingdom of God or the timing of the arrival of the apocalypse had to be modified.

In Matthew the date of this apocalypse was extended as he reports that God's rule is coming, while Luke slightly modifies the concept of the kingdom of God. However all three agree that this event will happen within the lifetime of their audience.

In Mark the central theme was the crucifixion, which was to occur to fulfill the scriptures and prove that Jesus was the Christ.

Over one-hundred verses are dedicated to the last hours of the life of Jesus.

The book of Matthew continues the concept of a fulfillment of the prophecies. In the story of the virgin birth he uses a phrase similar to; "to fulfill what was spoken," on five different occasions to prove to the Jews that Jesus was the Messiah.

Matthew also provides us with a very detailed genealogy in the first chapter that begins with Abraham and leads us all the way to Christ, the son of Joseph. This covers nearly forty generations and is designed to show that Jesus was a direct descendent from Abraham, as was written in the Old Testament.

Today many Christians use the NIV Bible, which states: *"Abraham was the father of Isaac, Isaac the father of Jacob, Jacob the father of Judah."* My family used the King James Version, which is still lauded for its beautiful use of the English language. In 1603, when King James ascended to the throne in Great Britain, illiteracy rates were extremely high. Therefore, most converts to Christianity would be exposed to the Bible and its teachings by hearing the words read, rather than actually reading. For this reason, the translators were instructed to beautify the language and make it sound like the word of God. The verses we read growing up during our daily devotions, following each meal stated, *"Abraham begat Isaac; and Isaac begat Jacob; and Jacob begat Judas."* My brothers and sisters referred to these verses as "the begats."

The fact that the NIV names do not match those in the King James version is of little interest to me. What caught my attention after several recitals of the begats evolved around the need for this genealogy in the first place. In the very same chapter, verse 18, Matthew states: *"Mary was pledged to be married to Joseph, but before they came together, she was found to be with child through the Holy Spirit."*

42

According to Matthew, Joseph was the father of Jesus in name only. It was not his sperm that impregnated Mary. What difference would it make who Joseph's father was, as he had nothing to do with the birth or conception. This genealogy does not provide a connection to Abraham, and I believe God would know that if he were the author.

The book of Matthew was written approximately 80 CE after the Jewish rebellion against Rome and the destruction of Jerusalem and the Temple. Matthew was attempting to convert the Jews to Christianity, and showing that Christ was the Messiah predicted in the Old Testament created a continuation of Judaism instead of conversion to a new religion.

The fulfillment of the prophecies added history to Christianity which has roots going all the way back to the creation story and the beginning of man. I believe that this is the reason for adding the virgin birth story to the book of Mark, which was one of his sources, and why there are so many references in Matthew using the phrase, "it is written," and why he continues to point out that an act was fulfilled as the prophets predicted.

There are multiple instances of Matthew adding dialogue to the story of Christ to demonstrate the fulfillment of the Scriptures that are absent from the other Gospel writers. Matthew alone has Jesus entering Jerusalem on a donkey, Judas sold for thirty pieces of silver, that he would be spat upon, beaten, and slapped, and that the disciples would desert him after his arrest. All of these were predicted by the Old Testament prophets like Isaiah and Zechariah.

The author of the book of Luke was apparently a disciple of Paul, and it is still the position of the church that this is the same Luke that is referred to in Colossians 4:14 as being a physician. Biblical scholars who study the authorship of the Bible doubt that he was a physician, or even a companion of Paul. The author wrote his books (Luke and Acts) a couple of decades after Paul wrote his letters, yet Luke does not seem to be aware of any of the letters written by Paul. Luke describes Paul as a Roman citizen and makes him much more hostile to the non-believing Jews. Paul actually taught in synagogues and teaches of the Jewish Messiah from the Jewish writings and chastises those that attempt to isolate the Jews. His message reported in his letter to the Romans clearly rejected the anti-Semitic approach to Christianity: Romans 11:1 *"Has God rejected his own people? Far from it."*

While Luke agrees with Matthew in the concept of the virgin birth, he does not explain it as part of the fulfillment of Old Testament prophecies. He instead explains that Christ was born the literal Son of God and that Mary was impregnated directly by God, which began his existence; this reflects a direct disagreement with John.

John disagrees with the other three Gospels in many aspects. He expresses no interest in the virgin birth and his book simply states that Jesus was and always will be by stating: John 1:14 *"The Word became flesh and made his dwelling among us."*

He was simply here as a grown man as he approached John the Baptist, who proclaimed him the "lamb of God."

As we discussed, John rarely uses the short phrases and parables but rather very long narratives which he attributes to Jesus. However, the most startling difference seen in John is his hostile view toward the Jews. The phrase "the Jews" appears over sixty times in the book of John. Where the Synoptic Gospels state that the "crowd" called for the killing of Jesus, John blames the "Jews." John also attempts to draw a distinction between Jesus and his disciples and the Jewish community by referring twice to "the Passover of the Jews," rather than simply the Passover. While the three Synoptic Gospels identify the differences Jesus had with the Jewish leaders, the Pharisees and scribes, John portrays a conflict with "the Jews."

The Synoptic Gospels maintain that the high priests, the elders and the crowd demanded that Barabbas, a murderer, be released

44

and that Jesus be crucified. John, on the other hand insists on several different occasions that it was the Jews that screamed, "Crucify!" and demanded that Jesus die. This anti-Semitism is most likely the reason John reports the condemnation of Judas, who was Jewish, by Jesus.

This anti-Jewish sentiment, expressed in the book of John, has caused some serious uneasiness within the Catholic Church to the point that a recent publication titled *Anti-Judaism and the Fourth Gospel* was written to address this problem. They concluded that the Fourth Gospel has a strong anti-Jewish element that is unacceptable from a Christian point of view but could not remove the anti-Jewish passages in an attempt to save the "healthy core of the message."

This must have caused great anguish within the Catholic Church. They were forced to either declare that Jesus was anti-Semitic or declare that at least the book of John was not an inerrant text. Religion forces some difficult choices.

Paul's writings were apparently written between the years 50 and 60, at least ten years before Mark. His writings indicate he had no access to the Gospels as he rarely discussed the life of Christ in any of his books. In fact, Paul makes no claims of miracles performed by Jesus, other than the resurrection, which is a rather significant exception.

While I was growing up, ministers used a common teaching tool that connected the writings of Paul to the Gospels. Paul often refers to earlier holy writings, and the ministers would claim that he was referring to passages found in Matthew or Luke. This is misleading because Paul did not have any of the Gospels available since they were written after his life. Any references to "holy writings" or statements regarding "as it is written," are references to the Torah, or Old Testament, the only holy writings available to him at that time.

Even though Paul never met Jesus and disagreed with his disciples on many key points of Christianity, his letters were significant. His books are the earliest surviving writings concerning Christianity and were written while some of Jesus' disciples were still alive and teaching. In fact, the writings of Paul predate the surviving Gospels by at least twenty years. His books are also the only surviving texts whose authorship is known. From his letters we are able to discern who he was and why he was writing.

How Do You Get Into Heaven?

While I was taught that there was only one way to get into heaven, the New Testament books are far from agreement on this critical question.

Matthew clearly states that the followers of Jesus must keep the Jewish Law. In chapter 5:17–20 he reports that Jesus stated he did not come to abolish the law of the prophets, but to fulfill them and that not one letter of the law will pass until all is accomplished. Keep in mind that his audience was primarily the Jewish community. For years before this book was written there was a significant disagreement between Paul and the apostle Peter regarding the requirement of circumcision of Christians. Paul was preaching to the gentiles and the idea of being circumcised was not a welcomed concept to the potential male converts.

In addition, like the Jewish faith, actions must accompany belief in Christ (Matthew 25:31–45). Those that get into heaven have given God food, drink, clothing, and cared for the sick. That which you do for the least of our brothers, you do for Jesus.

In chapter 19:16–22 Matthew tells the story of the rich man asking Jesus how to get into heaven. Jesus tells him to follow the commandments first, then give away his money and follow him.

Paul never suggested giving away money or performing any other acts of kindness to the poor. He taught that you only need to believe and follow Jesus. Paul believed that salvation was found only through believing in the death and resurrection of Christ, not by following Jewish Law or helping the poor.

What About the Book of Revelation and the Apocalypse?

The apocalypse, as reported in the book of Revelation, has always fascinated me and was a key component of the Baptist faith. According to Merriam-Webster the literal interpretation of the Greek word apocalypse is "to uncover" or "to reveal," hence the title, Revelation. The book of Revelation is one of a series of apocalyptic books and writings that predicts the end of the age when Satan's rule, through man, is destroyed. It predicts the return of Jesus, the imprisonment of Satan, the return of the dead, and the beginning of the New Earth.

The author of the book of Revelation identifies himself as John and explains that this God-inspired vision was given to him on the island of Patmos. There is significant discussion about John with some churches arguing that this is the same person as the author of the book of John. Either way, John of Patmos received this vision and writes the account as if he is viewing this total chaos and destruction from above.

Peter also authored a vision of the apocalypse and fragments of this document have been found recorded in both Greek and Ethiopian. This document is similar to the book of Revelation in that it records destruction of the world and a view of hell delivered to all non-believers.

The apocalyptic writings are a continuation of the message delivered by the teachings of earlier prophets like John the Baptist. John was the prophet that identified Jesus as the Messiah.

In the book of Mark, John the Baptist says that he is not the messenger everyone is waiting for, but he is there to prepare the way for the Christ. Compare the description of John the Baptist from Mark to the more apocalyptic Matthew: Mark 1:7–8 *"After me will come one more powerful than I, the thongs of whose sandals I am not worthy to stoop down and untie. I baptize you with water, but he will baptize you with the Holy Spirit."*

Mathew 3:11–12 *"I baptize you with water for repentance. But after me will come one who is more powerful than I, whose sandals I am not fit to carry. He will baptize you with the Holy Spirit and with fire. His winnowing fork is in his hand and he will clear his threshing floor, gathering his wheat into the barn and burning up the chaff with unquenchable fire."*

As a child, our church periodically brought in guest ministers who were very effective at describing the fire and brimstone that would await anyone who did not share his views of a Christian life. Enjoying anything that was produced by Satan including alcohol, rock music, playing cards, dancing, swearing, and attending movie theaters would immediately sentence you to eternal damnation and the fires of hell. It was a very effective message to a seven-year-old.

The idea of the triumphant return of Jesus, and eternal damnation to the non-believers, has gained significant attention with the *Left Behind* series of novels, written by Jerry Jenkins and Tim LeHaye, that depict the futuristic interpretation of Revelation where all Christians are taken up immediately into heaven and spared the chaotic destruction of the tribulation.

The book of Revelation is very difficult to read and nearly impossible to understand with its extensive use of numerology, the presence of the anti-Christ, unusual imagery, signs predicting the end of time, seven different cycles of the destruction, and the extensive use of metaphors. It is reminiscent of nightmares I had as a child, which could very well have been inspired by the message of those traveling evangelists.

The book of Revelation has several interpretations even within the Church. It was not unanimous that this confusing vision be considered inspired by God and worthy of inclusion in the biblical Canon. According to John Drane, in his book *An Introduction to the Bible*, Martin Luther "found it an offensive piece of work" and John Calvin "had grave doubts about its value." Thomas Jefferson, whom we will discuss in a later chapter, did not include anything about the apocalypse in his *Jefferson Bible* and wrote that he "considered it as merely the ravings of a maniac, no more worthy nor capable of explanation than the incoherence's of our own nightly dreams." It remains quite controversial to this day within the church and some denominations do not include it in their teachings.

The writings in the book of Revelation combined with some of the references attributed to Jesus regarding the "kingdom of God," or the similar phrase "kingdom of Heaven," are used to create a theology of anticipation of the end of the world. While most of us dread a nuclear holocaust or similar massive and final destruction of the Earth, some Christian theology teaches us to hope that this end occurs as soon as possible. This message is reflected in the bumper stickers proclaiming that the car will be unmanned in the event of the Rapture.

In Mark 13:5–37, the author provides a detailed description of the events that lead up to the final days. The author of Luke uses Mark and expands the series of events even more graphically (Luke 21:8–36). As we discussed in the basic rules of oral tradition, due to the length of this thirty-two-verse dialogue, it is extremely unlikely to reflect something Jesus actually said. It seems likely that the authors added this graphic depiction of the final days as a compelling story and an effective tool for conversion of the unbelievers.

Many agree that there would be merit in converting the unbelievers if it appeared that Jesus predicted the specific events regarding the destruction of Jerusalem prior to the actual occurrence. A more likely scenario is that this was added after the destruction of Jerusalem a few years prior to these writings. The scholars of the Jesus Seminar were nearly unanimous that Jesus did not speak these passages of the final days. They believed that this story was added because most of the story described the specific events that occurred during the fall of Jerusalem that occurred around 70 A.D. before this book was written. The authors of *The Five Gospels* explained their reasoning: "There is a striking correspondence between this passage and the description of the events preceding the Judean-Roman war of 66–70 C.E. by the Jewish historian Josephus, who wrote after the fall of Jerusalem. In his Jewish War he tells of phony prophets who led many astray, he depicts the famine that beset Jerusalem when the storehouses were burned. He narrates the burning of the temple and provides other parallels to Mark's little apocalypse."

When discussing the idea of an apocalyptic end to the world, Paul clearly did not teach that a series of signs would precede the coming of the kingdom of God. He stated in his letter to the Thessalonians 4:13–18 that the return of Jesus be sudden and unexpected like a "thief in the night."

A second letter to the Thessalonians, which is included in most Christian Bibles, lists a series of signs including a general rebellion and an anti-Christ figure which precludes the return of Jesus, has been determined by nearly all Biblical scholars to have been a forgery by an unknown author, not Paul.

Mark, Matthew and Luke agree that the kingdom of God would happen very soon.

Mark 12:34 *"You are not far from the kingdom of God."*

Matthew 10:7 *"The kingdom of heaven is near."*

Luke 10:11 *"The kingdom of God is near."*

Luke reports a conversation where the Pharisees ask Jesus specifically when the kingdom of God would come. Jesus replied;

Luke 17:20–21 *"The kingdom of God does not come with your careful observation, Nor will people say, 'Here it is,' or 'There it is,' because the kingdom of God is within you."*

The verse often gets overlooked in favor of the report of signs he describes in his mini apocalypse we discussed earlier.

Luke 21:31 *"Even so, when you see these things happening, you know that the kingdom of God is near."*

Since these two verses are not compatible, it is logical to me that this verse was added as part of the apocalypse story to encourage converts to decide quickly as the end is very near. Just like my minister used the book of Revelation.

Did Jesus teach about an apocalyptic end to the Earth? The earliest passages talked about the urgency to enter the kingdom of God, or Heaven. He spoke of the advantages of joining God in heaven and the attitudes and acts that would exclude you from joining him in this wonderful place.

We don't even know if it is a "place." For me personally, the Luke 17:20 verse is the most consistent with the life of Christ. It isn't here or there, it isn't following a cataclysmic destruction, it is "within you." You could attain your presence with God within yourself, well before your death, if you become like children;

Mark 10:14 *"He said to them, 'Let the little children come to me, and do not hinder them, for the kingdom of God belongs to such as these.'"*

Mark 10:15 and Luke 18:17 *"I tell you the truth, anyone who will not receive the kingdom of God like a little child will never enter it."*

In addition to opening your mind like a child, Jesus also directed us to give to the poor and attend to the sick, and you will be with God:

Luke 10:9 *"Heal the sick who are there and tell them, 'The kingdom of God is near.'"*

Luke 9:2 *"and he sent them out to preach the kingdom of God and to heal the sick."*

Matthew 19:21 *"If you want to be perfect, go, sell your possessions and give to the poor, and you will have treasure in heaven."*

Matthew 19:23 *"it is hard for a rich man to enter the kingdom of God...it is easier for a camel to go through the eye of a needle than for a rich man to enter the kingdom of heaven."*

Jesus is credited with using "the kingdom of God," or the "kingdom of heaven," over eighty times in the Gospels. The great majority of the time he uses them to explain what heaven would be like by the use of parables. The parables of the growing seed, the mustard seed, the sower, the great banquet, the ten minas, the hidden treasure and the pearl, the net, the ten virgins, and the workers in the vineyard are all used to describe the wonders of the kingdom of God.

Mark 12:27 *"Have you not read in the book of Moses, in the account of the bush, how God said to him, 'I am the God of Abraham, the God of Isaac, and the God of Jacob?' He is not the God of the dead, but of the living."*

After a brief examination of the origins of the Bible and the identity and possible motivation of the authors, it becomes easier to get a truer picture of Jesus using the limited resources we have.

The only "truth" that any of us have is the truth that is forged on the anvil of our soul. My truth may be entirely different than yours, but we need to make informed opinions based on the facts we have presented to us, rather than a myth that has been created and passed from generation to generation.

I have trouble accepting a religion that glorifies life after death. Our only guarantee is the breath we take this minute. As Christians, we need to appreciate every living moment, rather than hoping for a better life in heaven. Heaven may also exist after death, but why wait? The kingdom of God is within you. Help the infirmed, show understanding to those that are not like you, love your neighbor, give to the poor, learn to be more like the example that Christ gave us in his days here on Earth.

The books of the Bible were not inerrant. There are numerous inconsistencies, contradictions and errors throughout the Old and New Testament.

These same contradictions and errors eliminate an all-knowing God as the author of the Bible. If God is all-knowing, he wouldn't have created these inconsistencies. If God had moved the hands of the writers of these books, he has a very short and inconsistent memory.

My mother, God bless her, has a very convenient explanation when she explains, "God works in mysterious ways." If God dictates a book that is designed to show his greatness, his direction for salvation, and to tell the wonderful story of his son Jesus on Earth, yet fills it with errors and contradictions, I would maintain that God is more practical joker than mysterious. Sorry mother, I love you, but God is much greater than a practical joker.

I believe that these books were written by God-fearing men, who were so moved by the story of Jesus that they dropped all previous goals and responsibilities to allow them to record a story that changed the world. They did their best to record a story that had been handed down for generations, but their story was filled with minor discrepancies, inaccuracies, and told by men of very limited intellectual skills. There is no shame here, nothing for which to apologize, as they preserved pieces of the greatest story the Earth has ever seen.

We need to enjoy the stories as they may relate to our lives, and enjoy our living God. My God is a God for the living. Enjoy the God within you.

4

My God Is Bigger Than Your God

Why do so many Christians attempt to make God so small? Rather than embracing the infinite magnitude of God, they choose to limit his powers to finite illusions much like those of a Houdini. Or, as said many times, they make God in their own image. While I don't pretend to know the appearance of God, or to even begin to understand his enormity, I do know that he is far more magnificent than I can imagine.

Many of the classic gospel songs still make me tingle as I remember the sounds of the great singers of my childhood: Elvis's version of "How Great Thou Art" and the booming bass tones of the Blackwood Brothers singing "Give Me That Old Time Religion."

Give me that old time religion
Give me that old time religion
Give me that old time religion
It's good enough for me

It was good for my mother
It was good for my mother
It was good for my mother
and it's good enough for me.

Though it is still one of my favorite tunes, even with its simplistic lyrics, it evokes the Christianity of my youth that included a minister preaching segregation, fear, and denigration of people of color. It was a church of many false teachings. Catholics were idol worshipers. Jews were damned because they killed Jesus. And members of other Christian denominations—Methodists, Christian Reformed, Lutherans—were all going to hell. Only us Baptists, those who followed the *true* teachings of Jesus, were going to heaven.

I was confused. The Baptist church of my youth taught that the Bible was inerrant with every word inspired by God. Yet while my minister taught the word of God, his messages also contained references to white supremacy. What was I to believe? Was God a racist? Did God really want my Methodist friends and neighbors to burn in hell because they went to the wrong church? It became difficult for me to understand why the God I was expected to worship would want to sentence my friends to eternal damnation.

My study of the Bible showing discrepancies between the authors became impossible to overlook. Why would the God I worship, my God, not get these things right if his book was without error?

The book of Genesis, the story of the creation of man, is a fundamental cornerstone of the Christian religion. Researchers report that nearly sixty percent of Americans believe in the creation story as reported in Genesis.

Genesis is the primary basis for the fundamentalist Christian war against science. If one believes in the creation as written in Genesis it means disregarding the mountain of evidence regarding the survival of a species capable of adapting to its environment. One also has to completely disregard plate tectonics which teach us how mountains and valleys are formed, what causes volcanic eruptions, and why tsunamis occur. It means ignoring the incredible fossil records concerning species that existed prior to 4000 years ago. Not to mention the discovery of new solar systems, black holes, and other celestial wonders. In fact, the ideas of the revolution of our planet, and light being provided to Earth from the sun would also need to be discarded.

This is not a philosophical disagreement with the religious literalists. It is a war being waged against science by fundamental

Christians in the name of their religion. A war where every significant scientific discovery is denounced as "man attempting to play God."

According to Gallup, only sixteen percent of Americans read their Bible daily and only a small portion of that number have read the entire Bible, cover to cover. As the comedian Kathleen Madigan says: "Catholics don't read the Bible, they read the bulletin." The same could be said of most Christians. Biblical literacy in the United States has been diminished to reading an occasional verse, here and there, even though most Christians say the Bible guides their lives.

Yet, these same people enroll their children into Sunday school so they can be taught the story of creation as written in Genesis.

It takes most people less than five minutes to read the entire creation story in Genesis from beginning to end, though it takes a little longer to read it critically.

In many localities, educators are being asked to add the creation story to their science curriculum. If the story of creation, as reported in Genesis, is to be added to our classrooms then it is encumbered upon us to read the story critically so it will hold up to critical peer review.

Let's take some time to examine the story of creation, as recorded in the NIV version of Genesis 1.

"In the beginning God created the heavens and the Earth. Now the Earth was formless and empty, darkness was over the surface of the deep, and the Spirit of God was hovering over the waters."

As a teen I attempted to envision a "formless Earth," composed primarily of water. It is still difficult for me, but as a teenager in the sixties, my imagination drew me to our eighth grade science experiments with mercury.

Most people under the age of forty would find it hard to believe that those of us who were teenagers in the sixties were given small vials of mercury in our science class, while we chewed on our lead pencils. We were allowed to play with this toxic substance on our lab tables, and even bring it home. When you put your finger in the middle of your puddle of mercury, it would immediately break into numerous little puddles. With a gentle nudge, the little puddles would easily return to one big puddle. It's a shame that mercury is so toxic, thereby robbing all future generations of an entertaining afternoon. But those were different times and since then we've learned about the toxic properties of mercury.

A more recent vision of a formless Earth, is that of the astronauts playing with water in space, with tiny blobs of water floating around the International Space Station. Maybe that was what the Earth first looked like.

The vision of darkness being only over the surface of the deep begs a question. Is the deep the ocean, since later on God created dry ground? It is hard to imagine darkness over the deep as he had yet to create light. If darkness was only over the deep, what was over the rest of the Earth? This language is very confusing and it isn't helpful for a scientific theory to be so vague.

"And God said, 'Let there be light,' and there was light. God saw that the light was good, and he separated the light from darkness. God called the light 'day' and the darkness he called 'night.' And there was evening and morning—the first day."

It is a proven fact that the Earth rotates and the sun is constant. There is no "on" and "off" switch that creates light areas and dark areas in the universe. We also know that darkness is the absence of light. This story makes a tremendous amount of sense for someone living during the time this book was written. At that time everyone believed the Earth was flat. With a flat Earth, a logical explanation would be to have a light switch to create a day and night. This scientific theory only makes sense prior to the discovery of the Earth as a sphere that rotates around the sun. To believe that God wrote the creation story is to worship a God that has less knowledge of the solar system than the average third-grader.

The last sentence is a reflection of the Jewish tradition of what constituted a day. The day does not begin at daybreak, but rather at sunset. This is why the Sabbath is celebrated beginning Friday at sunset.

"And God said, 'Let there be an expanse between the waters to separate water from water.' So God made the expanse and separated the water under the expanse from the water above it. And it was so. God called the expanse 'sky.'"

Upon first reading, I thought the "expanse" would be land, as it clearly separates oceans, rivers and lakes. Calling the expanse the sky immediately reverses this concept. Could God be referring to the moisture in the clouds? In ancient times, some people believed that large bodies of water were present above the clouds, which caused rain to fall. This is in direct conflict with our understanding of the universe. We know, of course, that water is a very precious commodity for sustaining life, and only recently have we found possible evidence of water on any other planet, let alone large floating oceans in the sky.

"And God said, 'Let the water under the sky be gathered to one place, and let dry ground appear.'"

We know that water covers seventy-one percent of our planet Earth, however, at the time of this writing, the entire concept of "Earth" was primarily the land in the Middle East and Europe. It is interesting that God did not cause the land to rise causing the formation of mountains, hills and valleys. Instead of using gravity, which was a useless theory at the time since the Earth was considered flat, he gathered the water in one place.

"Then God said, 'Let the land produce vegetation: seed-bearing plants and trees on the land that bear fruit with seed in it, according to their various kinds.'"

This concept of life omits spores, molds, microscopic creatures, viruses, and bacteria and includes only vegetation that is seed-bearing. For that time, it was very inclusive, considering the limited knowledge of man at the time of this writing. Instead of making a case that God wrote this story, it illustrates the limitation of the knowledge of man at that time and religion blames this lack of man's knowledge on God.

"And God said, 'Let there be lights in the expanse of the sky to separate the day from the night, and let them serve as signs to mark seasons and days and years, and let them be lights in the expanse of the sky to give light on the Earth.' And it was so. God made two great lights—the greater light to govern the day and the lesser light to govern the night. He also made the stars."

Imagine sitting in a science class, and the teacher is explaining to you that on the first day of the creation of the Earth God made light, but he did not create the sun until the fourth day. The teacher would then continue to explain that the moon was the lesser light God gave us for night. Hopefully, there would be several weeks before the teacher explained that man has walked on the moon so that you would not connect the two. God knows that the moon is not a "light," and so do all of you. Men that lived a couple thousand years ago would find the biblical account very plausible given their understanding of the universe. As of this point in this scientific theory, not any part is sustainable to even the most basic scrutiny.

"And God said, 'Let the water teem with living creatures, and let birds fly above the Earth across the expanse of the sky.' So God created the great creatures of the sea and every living and moving thing with which the water teems, according to their kinds, and every winged bird according to its kind."

Clearly, this is not a controversial passage for the fifth day of creation. This is very inclusive by creating every living and moving thing in the water.

"And God said, 'Let the land produce living creatures according to their kinds; livestock, creatures that move along the ground, and

wild animals, each according to its kind.'... 'Let us make man in our image, in our likeness, and let them rule over the fish of the sea and the birds of the air, over the livestock, over all the Earth, and over all the creatures that move along the ground.'"

The sixth day was very eventful with the creation of livestock, creatures that crawl on the ground, wild animals, and man and woman. It is interesting that livestock is separate from wild animals. This informs us that all the animals that are used for labor and farming (sheep, goats, horses, cows, chickens, etc.) were essentially created and waiting for man to put them in their pens. There is no participation of man in the domestication of the animals.

This is the part many fundamental Christians want us to believe, that God created these things on a single day, including man in his present form, in the image of God. Without any basic evidence, in the middle of a story that shows the most crude and primitive understanding of nature, this report of the creation of animals and man has to be taught as a valid "scientific theory."

To any unbiased observer with a working knowledge of basic science, this is obviously a story created by men in an effort to establish the presence and authority of God. Six days of very hard work for an omnipotent God that left him exhausted and in need of a day's rest. This would be a Herculean effort for a man, but for an all-powerful God it would not raise a sweat.

I do not intend to demean those who believe in the creation theory as taught in the Bible. However it is difficult for any thinking educated person to believe that this is the way our world was created without making some tremendous exceptions or inventing some elaborate explanations.

This is the "science" my parents and grandparents were taught, and believed, in church. This is the same "science" I was encouraged to believe and embrace. This is the creation story that many Christians are pushing to include in a science curriculum in our schools. Why would this clearly fictitious story have the same scientific standing as the theory of gravity or relative motion? It is the "Old Time Religion" of my parents that I simply cannot embrace even though I still love to sing the song.

I would like to offer a different version, one that is much grander, much larger, and much more God-like.

In the beginning was a singularity. A singularity so tiny, that you couldn't possibly see it. In fact about 1,000,000,000,000 of them could fit on the dot of this "i." Can you imagine this? No, you can't. It is so incredibly small our minds can't possibly grasp it. Inside this singularity is packed every particle of matter needed to create every planet, person, building, animal and star in the universe.

Now, God decides to use this singularity and create an enormous explosion and in a split second this singularity spreads at least a hundred billion light years across, and is arranged in the universe in an order for the creation of stars, galaxies, and planets, one of which is Earth.

Incredibly enough, over an unknown number of years, Earth becomes an absolutely perfect environment to nurture and populate with a multitude of animals, birds, fishes, microorganisms, viruses, and every life form. Every aspect of this planet was in perfect proportion with the perfect mixture of oxygen, carbon dioxide, and other elements, the proper distance from the fiery ball of gas called the sun, and the exact amount of gravity to sustain life as we know it.

This planet is populated with a manner of life that changes to every situation that has arisen including periods of extreme cold, eruptions, and collisions with asteroids traveling at incredible speeds and covering half the planet in a cloud of dust. These life forms continue to make minor changes to survive and modify their way of sustaining life moving toward a much higher lifestyle, and culminating in the highest form of life, modern man.

From the singularity that is so tiny we cannot grasp its infinitesimal size, this God created a universe so vast and so grand that it too, is beyond comprehension. If you think you really understand the vastness of the universe, consider this fact: the average distance between the stars we are able to see through high-powered telescopes in our galaxy, the Milky Way, is twenty million-million miles. It is estimated that there are more than a billion stars in the Milky Way, and the Milky Way is just one of 140 billion galaxies resulting in a vastness of the universe that is unimaginable.

It would take a huge God to create this system. A God much greater than most could ever imagine. That is the God I worship. You cannot convince me that God is hiding up in the clouds and performing tricks like a street corner magician.

This, of course, is the Big Bang Theory, with God as the initiator. Promoting this places me in the precarious position of being lumped with the popular movement commonly referred to as "intelligent design." Unfortunately, most of the proponents of intelligent design are using the term to replace creationism, and attempting to posit this concept as a scientific theory. I do not share their goal. I agree with scientists that this evolution of our Earth took approximately 4.5 billion years and that life forms evolved in small steps to adapt to their environment. In other words, I believe in the survival of the fittest and the common ancestors of all surviving species. How my beliefs differ is that I believe God played a role. I can't prove it, but it is what I believe.

Even the title, the "Theory of Evolution" causes pseudo-intellectual discussions. The common perception of "scientific theory" is seriously distorted. Creationists attempt to diminish the theory of evolution by stating that it is "only" a theory. I certainly understand the confusion. In common language, the word "theory" infers a guess or hunch.

In science there are theories and facts. Facts are the world's data. For example, it is a fact that we have found skulls that appear to be intermediary steps between one species and another. Theories are structures of ideas that explain and interpret facts. Therefore, facts are not a higher standard than a theory, and the theory of evolution utilizes all available facts to construct a logical conclusion. Facts don't go away when scientists debate rival theories to explain them. Einstein's theory of gravitation replaced Newton's in the last century, but apples didn't suspend themselves in midair, pending the outcome. A theory is an explanation or model based on observation, experimentation, and reasoning, especially one that has been tested and confirmed as a general principle helping to explain and predict natural phenomena. This means that the proposed theory must be published in a legitimate scientific journal in order to provide the opportunity for other scientists to evaluate the relevant factual information and publish their objections. A theory is valid as long as there is no evidence to dispute its conclusions. The theory of evolution has withstood this intense scrutiny for over 100 years.

Let me be absolutely clear, my perceived role of God's involvement in the creation of the universe does not meet the requirements of a valid scientific theory as it adds the concept of a single creator without supporting evidence. Nor does it belong in a school curriculum. It would be appropriate for use in Sunday school, or included in a sermon. While it does attempt to harmonize God with science, it is not science.

During the discussions that lead to the Kansas State Board of Education requiring the teaching of intelligent design as an equal alternative to evolution in science classes, a very creative challenge emerged. To make intelligent design appear scientific, the developers of intelligent design never referred to the "designer" as God. In his very clever satire, *The Church of the Flying Spaghetti Monster*, author Bobby Henderson created a religion. His "church" taught that his Flying Spaghetti Monster was in fact the designer of the Earth and all living creatures. His pseudo-religion provided the same level of verifying evidence as those of the intelligent design movement, and he petitioned to be included in the science curriculum.

I would not want a science teacher to include the concept of the Flying Spaghetti Monster, the teacher's concept of how God created the universe, or the creation story to my children under the pretense of science, even if it coincides with my belief.

We need to leave science to the scientists and not contaminate God in our science classes. Teach children your religious beliefs at home, in church, and in the way you live. Keep the two separate and in the proper environment.

A serious problematic area for the proponents of creation is the fossil records available to all of us. It is estimated that nearly ninety-nine percent of all the species that once lived on Earth have become extinct.

Our fossil records have been growing tremendously in the past century. Even with these new discoveries, some serious "gaps" are still present. The fossil record does not provide a fluid record of "A" produced "B" which produced "C." Instead, we are left to fill in the spaces between specimen "B" and "E." What did "C" and "D" look like? These gaps in the fossil record have been used to discredit the entire theory of evolution by its critics. It has been argued by authors such as Richard Dawkins in his wonderful book *The Greatest Show on Earth: The Evidence for Evolution* that these gaps are actually very useful to our society as we would have a terrible time actually naming species without these gaps between common ancestors. There is actually very little genetic variation between most species on this Earth.

What most people don't realize is that it is actually very difficult to become a fossil. Most animals that die are generally consumed by other creatures.

My wife and I marvel at the interactions in our saltwater reef aquarium, and over the years we have seen the disappearance of numerous fishes, shellfish, and corals. Literally within days, the other fish, the sea stars, snails, and crabs have left no trace of the dead creature. As a wildlife enthusiast, I have watched a carcass of a large deer literally disappear, bones and all, within one year.

In order to become a fossil, the animal or person must die in an area that leaves an imprint, become covered rather quickly to preserve it from decay and animals, and become compressed and encased in solid rock. Then millions of years later, someone has to be digging in precisely that spot to find it. It is estimated that if the entire population of the United States (over 310 million people) died today, fewer than 200 single bones—less than an entire human skeleton—would be found over the course of a million years.

The fact that we have uncovered so many fossils is incredible. Every day Christians pass through natural history museums and marvel at the skeletons of Tyrannosaurus Rex, and the majestic Brontosaurus never stopping to wonder about the conflict these remains present to the basic premise of their religion.

While growing up, my minister echoed what I believe is the most creative response to the fossil record conflict with the Bible. Although he didn't use the term, he explained the concept developed by Philip Henry Gosse called the Omphalos hypothesis. Gosse argued that in order for the world to function, God must have created the Earth with mountains, and canyons, trees with growth rings, and fossils to give it the appearance of age. Rabbi Dovid Gottlieb gave a similar argument in *The Age of the Universe* when he wrote; "The bones, artifacts, partially decayed radium, potassium-argon, uranium, the red-shifted light from space, etc. all of it points to a greater age which nevertheless is not true." Some have even taken the Omphalos hypothesis a step further to suggest that the Earth could have been created yesterday and God planted our memories to make it appear to us that we had a history. This explanation requires a God that would be entirely intent on deceiving humans. What would be the purpose of such a grand scale deception from a loving God?

The concept of creation is not a valid scientific theory. As recorded in Genesis, it is beyond logic and clearly a story designed to explain the question, "Where did we come from?"

While Henderson's Flying Spaghetti Monster was a ridiculous alternative, his charts and stories were every bit as compelling to the scientific community as those arguments for intelligent design. Each falls apart under scientific scrutiny. As a Christian with a deep personal belief in God, I am not comparing this ridiculous satirical religion with the almighty God. I am stating that I believe that neither deserves time in our classrooms disguised as science.

As Christians, why don't we embrace a God that is capable of creating a universe beyond our imagination? Just like the title of Rich Mullins' classic song, "My God is an Awesome God."

PART TWO
The Church and Contemporary Issues

Alternative and progressive thoughts on some of the most conten-
tious issues facing organized religion today. Each will be discussed
from the context of the biblical content as presented in the previous chapters.

5

Religious Expression in the Public Arena

School Prayer and the Ten Commandments

For those of us who attended public schools in the 1950s and 60s, we remember our school day beginning with the principal giving announcements over the public address system and then ending with a prayer. During those days it was common to have a plaque containing the Ten Commandments prominently displayed down the hall near the entrance of the school. Neither is allowed on school grounds today.

Back then, popular opinion has it that all of the students played together as one, crime was non-existent, there were no gays or lesbians, and abortions never happened because everyone was abstinent. At home every child had two loving and caring parents who provided everything a child would need. *Ozzie and Harriet* was not just a popular television show during that era, it also provided aspirations about how everyone was supposed to live.

Funny how life looks in the rearview mirror when witnessed through the prism of a reality that never existed.

I was recently reminded of these so-called golden years while watching a prominent televangelist. His point was that the imagined dreamland of those days disappeared when the Christ haters made us stop praying in the schools and removed the Ten Commandments plaque which is obviously leading us toward a Sodom-like destruction.

My actual memories of elementary school during that era differ from what common knowledge would want us to believe. It was a time I would not want to repeat, nor would it be something I would want my children or grandchildren to experience. I remember students physically beating a teacher to the point of hospitalization and the common use of corporal punishment against students by teachers. Though I don't specifically recall anyone getting an abortion, I do remember a couple of young women whose boyfriends drove them across the state to Detroit or across the bridge into Canada for the weekend. There were several young women who went to live with a "relative" for a few months. Homosexuals were certainly not in view, but there were a couple of guys who were routinely tortured both physically and mentally by members of the football team, as the teachers turned their heads. This was at a time when we routinely hid under our desks during air raid drills in the ridiculous hope that those old wooden desks would protect us from nuclear fallout.

I actually remember the day when my school district was forced to discontinue our principal's morning prayer. Ironically, the action was led by our Baptist church and joined by the Methodist congregation shortly after the school district hired a Catholic principal. They feared the principal might direct his prayer to the Blessed Virgin Mary. After all, they said, it was important to protect the integrity of our faith.

Fearing the integration of Catholics into our school made as much sense as pretending that our desks would protect us in the event of a nuclear attack.

As a Christian, any call for prayer in schools is very alarming to me. My primary concern is that it violates one of the basic teachings of Christ that seems to be entirely overlooked by many in the evangelical community; how to pray: Mathew 6:5 *"And when you pray, do not be like the hypocrites, for they love to pray standing in the synagogues and on the street corners to be seen by men."*

Matthew 6: 6–7 *"But when you pray, go into your room, close the door and pray to your Father who is unseen. Then your Father, who sees what is done in secret, will reward you. And when you pray, do not keep on babbling like pagans, for they think they will be heard because of their many words."*

The thought of students listening to their principal praying over the PA system seems to violate Christ's own directive. Christ taught us how to pray and gave us the words to use. His prayer was much different than what is often heard in locker-rooms prior to football games. Is God really on the side of one team over another? Let's be real.

It is no wonder recent polls show a significant decline in Americans who profess to be Christian. When politicians and church leaders routinely throw around their Christian faith as a cloak to protect society from their evil opponent, rather than draw people to faith, they have the opposite effect of stirring their core constituencies while repelling those who do not agree away from Christianity. As a Christian I am embarrassed by all their chest pounding and blatant disregard for the directions Jesus gave us for modest and private prayer.

The daily prayers recited when I was a child did not solve our social issues and our society was far from the Christ-driven utopia some erroneously report. Racism was blatant and encouraged, sexual harassment of young women was common by both teachers and students, and intolerance for anyone that was "different" was common.

While I understand conceptually that displaying ten rules of conduct dictated directly by God would be a great basis for any society, I do not understand how the Ten Commandments, as reported in the Old Testament, apply to our judicial system or how they relate to our schools. I agree that the Ten Commandments are a solid basis for understanding the Christian and Jewish faiths, but as we briefly review each of these commandments, I encourage you to evaluate each one and decide if it should be a foundation for our legal system or if it would improve our educational programs.

You may recall, the original version was engraved on stone tablets by God and given to Moses on Mount Sinai. Moses carried them down to the Israelites who were in the midst of a celebration that included worshiping a golden calf. When Moses came down from the mountain and saw the commotion, he threw the stone tablets to the ground breaking them to pieces. Then Moses went back up the mount, and a forgiving God etched a new set of tablets.

These tablets were so important to God that he directed Moses to design a chest, or ark, in which to store the tablets. He was very specific on the size, materials, and outside design. The resulting Ark of the Covenant was "two and a half cubits long, a cubit and a half wide, and a cubit and a half high," which is approximately 4 feet x 2 ½ feet x 2 ½ feet.

Unfortunately, through the many travels of the Ark and the destruction of the temple in Jerusalem, the actual tablets have been lost though the content lives on in the Bible.

Discussions regarding the value of posting the Ten Commandments prominently in our schools or court buildings reveal that most of us are unable to name, even in general terms, more than three of the ten. To accurately evaluate the value of displaying these documents, it would be helpful to first review what each commandment says in order to make a logical decision of their suitability for display.

The Ten Commandments begin in Exodus, chapter 20, verse 2:

First Commandment: *"I am the lord your God, who brought you out of the Egypt, out of the land of slavery. You shall have no other gods before me."*

This admonition is to remind the Israelites that they should avoid the multitude of other pagan gods that were commonly worshiped at that time. As most of us are not descendants of the Israelites, technically, God did not bring me or my ancestors out of Egypt. While this is important for display in a church building and provides a historical reminder of the plight of the Israelites, is it suitable or even important in a public school or court building?

Second Commandment: *"You shall not make for yourself an idol in the form of anything in heaven above or on the Earth beneath or in the waters below. You shall not bow down to them or worship them; for I, the Lord your God, am a jealous God, punishing the children for the sin of the fathers to the third and fourth generation of those who hate me, but showing love to a thousand generations, of those who love me and keep my commandments."*

This verse can be disturbing to some and is often misunderstood. The idea of a jealous God can be a bit frightening unless understood in the context in which it was written. It seems very inappropriate to indicate that any crime that you may commit will result in the punishment of your children for the next three or four generations. Why would one want such a controversial and misunderstood document posted in a school or courthouse? The Second Commandment is not a premise for our judicial system, nor a founding principle of our educational system.

Third Commandment: *"You shall not misuse the name of the Lord your God, for the Lord will not hold anyone guiltless who misuses his name."*

The King James Version uses more familiar language when it prohibits using the "Lord's name in vain." Whichever phrase is used, many scholars believe that this is a prohibition against misrepresenting what God teaches as well as using his name in a profane manner. While we strive to refrain from the practice, it is not a founding legal principle and is obviously a direct contradiction with the Bill of Rights.

Fourth Commandment: *"Remember the Sabbath day by keeping it holy. Six days you shall labor and do all your work, but the seventh day is a Sabbath to the Lord your God. On it you shall not do any work, neither you, nor your son or daughter, nor your manservant or maidservant, nor your animals, nor the alien within your gates. For in six days the Lord made the heavens and the Earth, the sea, and all that is in them, but he rested on the seventh day. Therefore the Lord blessed the Sabbath day and made it holy."*

While it is good to take time off and rest, it is clearly not illegal to work on the Sabbath. This commandment also repeats the creation story which is contrary to a central premise of our geological and natural history sciences. This commandment is contrary to both our legal system and our educational principles and would be inappropriate for display in either.

Fifth Commandment: *"Honor your father and your mother, so that you may live long in the land the Lord your God is giving you."*

To honor your father and mother is certainly a part of all civilized cultures and it is not surprising that God would command that you honor them. While giving honor to your father and mother is critical to a healthy and loving family, in our society families break up. Sometimes there is abuse involved. It is not, nor should it be, a crime to leave your parents and disagree when the parent acts in a criminal or abusive manner. Surely, while an ideal, it is not appropriate for posting in a public building.

Sixth Commandment: *"You shall not murder."*

This obviously is a critical part of our judicial system and against the law in all fifty states, with or without a plaque of the Ten Commandments posted on the wall.

Seventh Commandment: *"You shall not commit adultery."*

Clearly, adultery is a violation of your marital vows and of the faith each spouse places in their relationship, but it is not a crime. It has no place in our court system. This commandment would be appropriate for inclusion in the social sciences along with being honest, honoring all commitments, and understanding your role in a greater community.

Eighth Commandment: *"You shall not steal."*

While this is both a good rule and solid basis for a judicial system, it is already covered by the laws of the court and of society.

Ninth Commandment: *"You shall not give false testimony against your neighbor."*

Clearly, lying under oath is a crime which is punishable within the court system. Distorting stories, spreading gossip, passing lies or partial truths concerning your friends and neighbors may be wrong or immoral, but it is not against the law.

Tenth Commandment: *"You shall not covet your neighbor's house. You shall not covet your neighbor's wife, or his manservant or maidservant, his ox or donkey, or anything that belongs to your neighbor."*

Merriam-Webster defines covet as "desire," or "to wish for enviously." While being envious is not a good trait, it is not against the law nor does it belong as any part of our education system or judicial system.

To review: Of the Ten Commandments, only two are crimes in all fifty states. The ninth, giving false witness, is only a crime while testifying in court.

Now ask yourself, why in the world is it so important that we would mandate, or even allow this religious document to be displayed in our courts or taught in our schools?

Clearly, the values that are taught in our schools, as well as every part of our judicial system, reinforce the prohibition against stealing and killing. We, like the Israelites and every civilized society, are well aware that these actions are inconsistent with a functioning society and our faith in God.

The tradition of the Ten Commandments and their place in historical Christianity and Judaism is, without question, important and meaningful. Why taint their importance through laws, mandates and public displays?

6

Religion in Our Private Lives

Marriage and Divorce

A topic that has received a lot of attention of late is same-sex marriage. The conservative Christian community uses several quotations to condemn homosexuality in general, and a few select verses to oppose these marriages. While most would assume that the traditional marriage between heterosexual couples is well founded in the Bible, a closer look reveals numerous examples of non-traditional concepts of marriage. Unlike the issue of homosexuality, where Christ was silent, Jesus had quite a lot to say about marriage, adultery, and divorce.

There are numerous stories in the Old Testament that demonstrate a very lenient concept of marriage. There are repeated examples of respected biblical men that took several wives and concubines that sometimes numbered into the hundreds. Many of the characters in the Old Testament, including Moses, took a second wife.

Jesus does not take a position regarding the issue of polygamy. Mark 10:7 tells us: *"For this reason a man will leave his father and mother and be united to his wife, and the two will become one flesh. So they are no longer two, but one."* While this defines what the union of marriage is in his eyes, it does not say that only one union can happen at a time. In fact, some very conservative Christian denominations, including Jesus Christ of Latter Day Saints, practiced polygamy.

It is interesting that many marriage ceremonies look to Paul for quotations to be recited at weddings. Paul clearly had a very unusual view of marriage, and is not someone that I would consider for marriage counseling.

The Bible is very clear that the apostle Paul never married, and took great pride in the fact that he did not need, nor desire a wife. He clearly states his preference in saying: *"It is good for a man not to marry. But since there is so much immorality, each man should have his own wife, and each woman her own husband. The husband should fulfill his marital duty to his wife"* (I Corinthians 7:1–3). He continues: *"Now to the unmarried and the widows I say: It is good for them to stay unmarried, as I am. But if they cannot control themselves, they should marry, for it is better to marry than to burn with passion."* (I Corinthians 7: 8–9)

According to Paul marriage is reserved for those without proper self-control and that any relationship between a husband and wife is not to be about romance but simply to fulfill the marital duty.

Paul goes on to counsel, *"But if you do marry, you have not sinned; and if a virgin marries, she has not sinned. But those who marry will face many troubles in this life, and I want to spare you this."* (I Corinthians 7:28)

Continuing in verse 29, *"From now on those who have wives should live as if they had none; those who mourn, as if they did not; those who are happy, as if they were not."*

In summary, he seems to be saying if you are too weak to practice complete self control, be prepared for a terrible lifetime of trouble and even if your spouse dies you shouldn't mourn their death; simply accept the fact and move on. For those unfortunate souls that are happy in marriage, it is much better to pretend that you are miserable. Not exactly the kind of counseling most couples would want. These verses often come to mind as I am listening to the more frequently used quotations from chapter 13 by the same author.

Perhaps Paul is not the best spokesperson for love, romance and the sanctity of marriage.

A more interesting take on marriage is provided in Mark 10:9 that is central to the topic of marriage in our society. In this familiar quotation: *"Therefore what God has joined together, let man not separate."* Or as the King James Bible says: *"Let not man put asunder."* (KJV).

The act of marriage in a church is both a legal union as well as a religious ceremony, symbolizing joining together before God. In this ceremony, the minister, priest, or rabbi is declaring your union before God, asking for God's blessing on the marriage, and joining you together in God's graces.

What about civil marriages? Those that take place at the local courthouse, on a ship, or even a drive thru in Las Vegas? While recognized by most protestant churches, they are not legal unions in the Catholic Church which does not acknowledge any union unless performed by a priest.

In the case of same-sex marriages, I believe they should be held up to the same standards as a union between a man and woman. If the union is between two loving individuals (same sex or not) then the minister should perform the ceremony. Ministers routinely base their decision on pre-marital counseling. If the couple does not meet their pastoral standards then the minster should not have any obligation to unite the couple. Currently there are no laws in any state prohibiting the minister from making this decision, nor should there be.

Likewise, the state should never interfere with a minister's decision to unite two individuals who meet their theological standards.

The issue is not same-sex marriage. Rather the issue is same-sex civil unions. Following a marriage ceremony, the clergy must complete state-mandated forms to verify the union of the two participants. When this form is recorded, the couple is now joined in a religious and legal union recognized by the state.

Many, including the apostle Paul, have made the argument that marriage is designed so that the species can multiply. If that is the only reason for marriage, as Paul professed, then fertility tests should be required prior to every marriage.

As a Christian, and a follower of the teachings of Jesus, it is important to note that according to our written records, he never once mentioned homosexuality. Interestingly, Jesus did weigh in on the topic of divorce, which he was against. With nearly half its membership involved in divorce during their lifetimes, most Christian denominations conveniently overlook this condemnation. If one is looking for a "threat to the institution of marriage," which is often cited by opponents to gay marriage, maybe it needs to be more concerned with the heterosexual community. The threat to the sanctity of marriage is the increasingly high divorce rate.

As for the subject of divorce the Bible is used to both support the prohibition or condone the practice. Those of us who have gone through the extremely difficult experience of divorce can attest to the pain it causes. Often the members of one's own church will treat each party differently, either consciously or subconsciously. Many churches will actually assign blame or even send one of the former couple away as if to keep the divorce from infecting other members.

During Old Testament times divorce was not much of a concern. If a marriage was not working out, Mosaic Law stated that the man could simply discard his wife by writing a certificate of divorce. No courts, no custody battles, and no division of property. The man simply gives his wife a handwritten certificate and she is then forced to leave. It would seem that the Old Testament of the Bible not only condones divorce, it provides an express lane.

The New Testament provides two different views on divorce, both attributed to Jesus. Luke and Mark claim that Jesus taught that anyone who divorces his wife is committing adultery. By contrast, Matthew softens this statement from Jesus by allowing for divorce when marital unfaithfulness is the cause.

Unfortunately, all three books agree that if you are to divorce and remarry, that both you and your new wife, are committing adultery.

In Matthew 5:27, Christ addresses the act of adultery: *"You have heard that it is said, do not commit adultery."*

As we discussed earlier, John 8:4–11 tells the familiar story of the woman that the Pharisees drag to Jesus and ask that she be stoned because she was caught in the act of adultery. Jesus commands the accusers: *"If any one of you is without sin, let him be the first to throw a stone at her."* The remainder of the story is equally as instructive. As the accusers dropped their stones and left one-by-one, he then asks her, *"has no one condemned you?"* She explains that no one has. And Christ then states: *"then neither do I condemn you."*

The New Testament teaches that Christ believed that adultery was a sin and that divorce is an act of adultery, though he does reduce the punishment from death to simply being a sin.

President Jimmy Carter, a literalist Christian, confessed to adultery as taught in Matthew. His sin, you may remember, was that he had "lusted in his heart" for other women. This view of adultery is presented in Matthew 5:28: *"But I tell you that anyone who looks at a woman lustfully has already committed adultery with her in his heart."*

How many of us would make a similar confession? Under this definition most are probably guilty.

While the Gospels may seem harsh by today's standards, they are less extreme than Mosaic Law as followed in the Old Testament. Jesus disavowed this approach and made it clear that he disagreed with Mosaic Law. He said it did not fit the people who lived during the time of his ministry. Christ knew that Moses wrote the Mosaic Law specifically for a poorly educated, hardened people that had been enslaved prior to their years of searching the desert for the Holy Land. They were a traveling band that were attacked from all sides and attacked any community unfortunate enough to be in their way. It was critical that they keep this group together and not allow small groups to splinter off, as it would weaken the tribe. Mosaic Law worked for centuries as the Jewish people wandered through the wilderness.

As for same-sex marriage, the persecution and demonization of homosexuals has gone on long enough. The practice of using obscure and isolated passages to denigrate individuals who were created by God to love someone of the same sex, is a reflection of a hardened heart.

The argument against same-sex marriage has direct parallels to the prohibition against interracial marriages that existed in the U.S. for nearly three centuries. While it may seem hard to believe for anyone under the age of thirty-five, we have had laws against interracial marriages dating back to 1664. Not only did nearly every Christian church castigate it—in many states it was a crime to marry someone of a different race.

What possible justification was used to enforce this ban? The same reasons used to stop same-sex marriage.

First, it was contrary to God's will, as stated in Old Testament primarily in the books of Exodus and Leviticus based on the prohibition against marrying into another tribe.

Secondly, it was labeled as illicit sex rather than marriage. This allowed the states to charge the offenders with the crime of illicit and lewd behavior. This practice is very similar to the sodomy laws still in place in most states, even though no heterosexual couples would ever be prosecuted for anal sex.

The third argument was used repeatedly, as it is with gay marriage, that it was "unnatural." This argument, which seems like an incredible stretch today, was articulated in a declaration from the Supreme Court of Virginia in 1878: "The purity of public morals, the moral and physical development of both races... require that they should be kept distinct and separate... that connections and alliances so unnatural that God and nature seem to forbid them, should be prohibited."

What finally turned the public opinion on interracial marriage was a Christian group in California. The Catholic Interracial Council of Los Angeles joined with the ACLU and the Japanese American Citizens League to successfully argue that scientists no longer believed the differences between the races were "natural" nor "significant."

In his ruling, Justice Roger Traynor of the California Supreme Court stated: "The right to marry, is the right of individuals, not of racial groups." That argument was upheld in the United States Supreme Court in 1967 in Loving v. Virginia. That ruling provides us hope that the courts will eventually rule likewise on the issue of same-sex marriage.

Homosexuality

The life of a homosexual is very difficult. Who would ever purposely choose that lifestyle? I'm guessing not many. Seeing gays or lesbians engaging in simple acts of affection is often uncomfortable for those who are heterosexual. The recent movie, *Brokeback Mountain*, is a good example of confronting that discomfort. Yet those who are not gay, lesbian, or transgendered and have had the pleasure of socially meeting members of that community often come away with a great deal of respect and admiration for their courage in the wake of so many societal pressures against them.

Biologically, a union between a man and a woman is clearly more advantageous to the preservation of our species. Conveniently, it is also important for any subculture, such as a religious movement, that its members procreate and raise children that carry on the beliefs of that faith. I understand why a religion would prefer heterosexual relationships. Even on a personal level, having the opportunity of watching the birth of your child is an experience that changes your life.

As a couple, my wife and I are welcomed graciously by nearly everyone we meet as we travel around the world, attend celebrations together, worship together, and socialize in our community. I love the fact that we still hold hands, kiss when we greet or part, and can proclaim our love for one another regardless of the company.

In most communities across our country, and certainly in third world countries, homosexuality is not only against social norms, in many cases, it is against the law.

The more conservative churches tend to be more intolerant of the gay community. Some have gone so far as to outright condemn the practice, saying it does not belong in the Christian church.

The reason for this is simple. Many ministers and church leaders of the evangelical conservative church teach that sexual preference is a choice. Ignoring all of the science, which is consistent with their other beliefs, they proclaim that God will convert them to heterosexuality if they simply follow the teachings of the Bible.

Not only is this contrary to scientific studies, and is hurtful to the individual, it defies simple logic. I remember specifically when I decided to be baptized into the Baptist church just as clearly as I remember the day I decided to leave that faith. I remember my first "crush" on my second grade teacher, my first kiss from a girlfriend, and the moment I decided to propose to my wife, Irene. I do not recall making a choice to be heterosexual. Do you?

Every gay or lesbian individual that I have ever spoken with regarding his or her sexuality is able to relate the time that they realized they were homosexual, though none ever relate a story about "choosing" to be gay. Who among us would trade our lifestyle for one fraught with daily ridicule and rejection?

Apparently these same church leaders fail to listen to their own teachings that God does not make mistakes. Saying that those who are "choosing that lifestyle" could become heterosexual if they only returned to God and followed the teachings of Christ, are not following the same Christ I have found in my own study. Many gays that I have known have professed to be Christian, in spite of their treatment by the church. It confounds me that they would embrace a religion that so openly condemns them. Perhaps they understand the love of Christ better than we.

In the thousands of years since the writing of the Bible, science has provided us with a wealth of information regarding homosexuality. In the last thirty years research has shown us that homosexual orientation is as natural as heterosexual orientation from a physiological and psychological standpoint. Psychiatrists and physicians refuse to treat homosexuality, as it is not a disease of the body or mind. Yet, many in the Christian church, in their infinite knowledge, declare it to be an abomination.

When challenged by the wealth of scientific evidence, the conservative and fundamentalist pastors respond with the predictable phrase: "Let's see what God has to say about this." Then they refer to quotations from the book of Leviticus or Deuteronomy.

As we have previously discussed, it is my belief that attempting to read the Bible as the inerrant word of God is a difficult and futile task, due to the numerous contradictions and the persistent errors. While the books of the Old Testament are instructive of the incredible journey of the early Jewish peoples, it is difficult to find guidance for our personal lives from this series of ancient religious laws and stories.

For example, the book of Leviticus is a continuation of God's discussion with Moses on Mount Sinai. Moses ascended Mount Sinai to see God face-to-face and returned to the Israelites with the Ten Commandments. However, God did not stop there. He kept Moses there to discuss a multitude of issues. The God of the Israelites was very concerned with details concerning the Hebrew faith. For eleven chapters God tells Moses such things as how various offerings—such as the fellowship offering, the grain offering, sin offering, etc.—are to be prepared and executed.

God then presents Moses with a list of what are clean and unclean in his sight. If something was unclean, a sacrifice was in order, and forgiveness was demanded before that person could be declared clean. The condemnation of homosexuality is included in the list of unclean actions.

For those who believe that Leviticus reflects God's intentions for Christians, I would hope that their faith would require them to follow all of these condemnations consistently as a guide to their daily life and not just those that conveniently feed their prejudice.

The eleventh chapter of Leviticus tells us that the only meat we are allowed to eat must come from an animal that has a split hoof and that chews a cud. The meat must be cooked without containing any blood. Pork is eliminated as pigs do not chew cud. Rabbits do chew cud but do not have a split hoof. Creatures from the sea must have fins and scales which eliminates shrimp and lobster. That pretty much leaves beef and lamb.

For parents, sex after childbirth must wait until the mother is clean. For boys the mother is unclean for seven days. Before resuming sexual relations a sacrifice must be given; preferably a year-old lamb and a pigeon. Circumcision must be on the eighth day and then the couple must wait for thirty-three days prior to having sex. If the baby is a girl, the mother is unclean for two weeks, and then, after sacrificing a lamb and pigeon, the couple must wait sixty-six days.

Sex during the woman's monthly menstruation cycle is strictly forbidden. Violating this order requires the couple to be expelled from your community.

For business owners, employees must be paid each day, not weekly or every other week. Men's hair is not to be cut at the sides of his head nor can his beard be trimmed.

Leviticus 20:13 addresses the concept of homosexuality by stating: *"If a man lies with a man as one lies with a woman, both of them have done what is detestable. They must be put to death."*

Rather harsh punishment. Is this the punishment fundamental Christians want transgressors to receive? Unfortunately, this ancient law has been the justification for abuse including torture and even the murder of homosexuals, by Christians, for centuries.

In my youth I was subject to the screaming of a traveling evangelist during a sermon that homosexuals were an abomination and if discovered, they must be put to death. He continued that they would contaminate the faithful if allowed to live among us.

Leviticus 20:9 tells us: *"If anyone curses his father or mother, he must be put to death."*

As for adultery, verse 10 tells us, *"If a man commits adultery with another man's wife—with the wife of his neighbor—both the adulterer and the adulteress must be put to death."*

The same conservative Christians that are so quick to condemn homosexuals using the quotations from Leviticus choose to overlook these two condemnations that apparently warrant the same punishment. While this book clearly does condemn homosexual actions, many more verses are dedicated to teach us how to establish a fair price for our slaves.

The Mosaic laws were primarily established to determine the appropriate sacrifice for the nature of our sin. Using Mosaic Law to justify homophobia ignores a basic premise of nearly every Christian denomination—the concept of atonement—that Christ died for our sins as the ultimate sacrifice. How is this ancient record a guide for living in the twenty-first century?

Another well known and often cited story from the Old Testament regarding homosexuality involves the story of Sodom and Gomorrah. This is the story where God tells Abram to leave his home and the land of his father, and travel to a land that God will show him. In the story Abram, at seventy-five years of age, packed up his wife, his nephew Lot and their possessions and followed God to Canaan. When they arrived, Abram and Lot had a disagreement. Eventually Lot and his family leave to settle near Sodom. It was here that God told Abram, now ninety-nine years old, that God still has plans for him.

God tells Abram that he would be "very fruitful" and that he would be the father of all nations and now be called Abraham. His wife Sarai, would now be known as Sarah and would become pregnant with a son. In exchange, Abraham was to circumcise every male child from his family, "whether born in your household or bought with your money." Meaning even his slaves must be circumcised if they are to remain with the family.

God then informs Abraham that he is going to destroy all of Sodom and Gomorrah because their sins were so heinous. Abraham convinces God, through shrewd negotiations, the cities should be saved if he can find just ten righteous in their midst. A clever tactic since his nephew Lot was living there with his family, making the chances of finding a few other righteous men less difficult.

God sends two angels to visit Lot at his home in Sodom. Apparently God was right. We are told that all the men from every part of Sodom met outside Lot's house and demanded he send the two strangers out to the crowd of men, so they could have sex with them.

The story gets interesting when Lot goes outside to the men and begins his own negotiations by saying: *"No, my friends. Don't do this wicked thing. Look, I have two daughters who have never slept with a man. Let me bring them out to you, and you can do what you like with them."*

That is correct. Lot, the "righteous" nephew of Abraham, is confronted with a huge mass of men looking for a sexual encounter and he immediately offers to send them his two virgin daughters.

Amazingly, and fortunately for his daughters, the mob of men refuse the daughters but continue to demand the two strange men. Not only were the men heinous, every man in the village was apparently homosexual.

God tells Lot, his wife, and two daughters they must leave the city, whereupon God destroys the entire valley with burning sulfur. God instructs them to not look back, however, Lot's wife, who was weak, looks back. God immediately turns her into a pillar of salt.

This is usually seen as the end of the story, but the last part is also of great interest. It seems that Lot and his daughters settled in a cave. The daughters were worried that they would never find a husband and came up with a clever plan of their own. One night they served their father, Lot, enough wine to get him intoxicated and one of the daughters waited until he passed out, and engaged him in sex. The second daughter loved the plan and did the same thing the next night. Each became pregnant though their father was completely unaware of the entire episode and had no memory of the sexual encounters.

Apparently, after being rejected by an entire city of men and probably losing their self-confidence, Lot's daughters felt their only chance to have children was to rape their father.

There is certainly enough sin in the story of Sodom and Gomorrah for everyone. The troubling fact is that many Christian churches are more willing to overlook incest or giving daughters away to a raping mob, than homosexuality.

While many ministers choose to focus on the sins of homosexuality, when the story is later summarized in Ezekiel 16:48, the writer does not even mention homosexuality. Instead God listed the sins of Sodom to be: *"arrogant, overfed and unconcerned; they did not help the poor and needy. They were haughty and did detestable things before me."*

The real lessons of this story teach us not to commit mass rape or offer our daughters to an oversexed mob of men but rather to be humble before God and attend to the poor and needy.

Any discussion regarding homosexuality in the Old Testament would be incomplete without a mention of the love expressed between David and Jonathan as told in 1 Samuel, chapter 13 through 2 Samuel chapter 1. While there is no mention of lovemaking in their relationship, the homoerotic subtext of the story between Prince Jonathan and the beautiful and heroic David cannot be ignored: Samuel 16:12 *"And he sent, and brought him in. Now he was ruddy, and withal of a beautiful countenance, and goodly to look to. And the Lord said, Arise, anoint him: for this is he." (King James Version)*

New Testament references to homosexuality are found in the letters of Paul. In Romans 1:26, Paul is writing to the Romans following his trip throughout the Mediterranean. The trip included visits to areas governed by the likes of Nero and Caligula, who were both famous for their depraved life styles. He also visited Greece where the temples were filled with statues built to Aphrodite, and other goddesses of sex. The religious services witnessed by Paul focused primarily on pleasure, sex, lust, and passion and involved unusual rituals like orgies to honor the pagan gods. Paul's letter to the Corinthians appears to be in reference to this idol worship and same sex orgies: *"They have become filled with every kind of wickedness, evil, greed, and depravity."*

The next reference from Paul in 1 Corinthians 6:9–10 mentions "homosexual offenders" along with the sexually immoral, idolaters, adulterers, male prostitutes, greedy, drunkards, slanderers and swindlers together. It seems a bit disingenuous to isolate the homosexual offenders, or male child molesters, and equate that to a committed homosexual relationship.

As we see, references in the Bible regarding homosexual behavior are condemnations of immoral acts such as rape, orgies, idol worship, and child molestation. These references do not specifically condemn the act of people of the same sex loving each other in a monogamous and loving relationship.

As has happened throughout the history of the Christian faith, changes continually happen as Christianity adapts to trends in society. The literal understanding of the Bible no longer makes sense as we continue to evolve as a society, our knowledge of human nature increases, and our differences such as color, race, and religions begin to dissolve with the light of this knowledge.

As William Sloane Coffin, the former chaplain at Yale University has said, "In reality, there are no biblical literalists, only selective literalists." The church and each denomination have been making changes through oral teachings that have changed the emphasis on Christianity over the years.

Abortion

Abortion is a very difficult issue for many Christians, myself included.

In spite of the fact that abortions have been practiced throughout recorded human history, and were actually permitted under Roman law at the time of Jesus, the Bible does not make specific reference to abortion. Any attempt to find biblical guidance on this issue creates conflicting viewpoints and must be viewed from a proper biblical and historical perspective.

Members of both the pro-life and pro-choice groups attempt to use verses from the Old Testament to support their positions. Interestingly, both sides use this quote from Exodus 21:22–23 to support their positions: *"If people are fighting and hit a pregnant woman and she gives birth prematurely but there is no serious injury, the offender must be fined whatever the woman's husband demands and the court allows. But if there is serious injury, you are to take life for life ..."*

The Pro-choice community would claim that this passage decrees that causing the miscarriage, or abortion, was punishable by a fine. If further injury occurred to the mother, a penalty up to death was appropriate. They claim this indicates that the unborn did not receive the status of a human life.

Pro-life groups point out that injury or death to the unborn is to be punished, indicating that God values life before birth.

These scriptures were written as part of Mosaic Law handed down to Moses from God. As earlier noted, it is difficult to use Mosaic Law as a practical guide for the twenty-first century.

This same chapter in Exodus details how God wants you to treat your Hebrew slave, how and when to sell your daughter, and that anyone that curses his father or mother is to be put to death. Using this passage to argue any side of the debate, unless one also agrees with the extended passage, is not appropriate. It is difficult to apply selected Mosaic Laws to our lives.

Discussions on abortion hinge on the concept of when life begins. The pro-life community is adamant that the Bible is a valid reference and guide for settling this issue. Their central premise includes:

There is no reference anywhere in the Bible to a fetus, and all references state "boy child" or simply "with child."

The Bible teaches that life is found in the "blood" (Deuteronomy 12:23), and blood begins to flow through a fetus during the very early stages of fetal development.

God created only three classes of life—plant, animal, and people—therefore a child must belong to the category of man. This is reinforced by the phrase "with child," which is frequently used in the Bible.

In Psalms 51:5, the author states that David claimed to be *"sinful from the time my mother conceived me."* Since only humans can be sinful, the fetus must be human.

Abortion disannuls God's plan. If God allows a child to be conceived, he must have a plan for that child.

In order to discuss these arguments, an historical perspective is helpful.

First, the authors of the Old Testament had a very crude and basic understanding of life on Earth. The creation story has no accommodation for crustaceans, molds, and microscopic organisms. The writers clearly believed that other cultures were lower life forms, a philosophy which racists hold to this day.

Medical knowledge was practically non-existent. Nothing was known about viruses or bacteria, and the scientific understanding of the human body was completely incorrect.

Hundreds of years after Christ walked the Earth, it was still commonly thought that the heart was at the core of human intelligence with the brain primarily being its cooling system. Therefore it was understandable such high priority was placed on the heart as the muscular contractions could actually be felt and heard. To emphasize the importance of the heart, most deaths in those times occurred due to injury resulting in the loss of blood. It is easy to understand this belief as it is rather obvious that the heart is driving the blood through our body and severe blood loss results in death—a crude misunderstanding of human anatomy resulting in the heart being the most critical organ. The brain, on the other hand, was simply a mushy substance without moving parts or any obvious function.

From this perspective it is easy to understand why the early Hebrews did not have a term for fetus. While the term "with child" is rarely used any longer, it reflects the understanding that the only option for a live, naturally-conceived birth is a human offspring. Saying my dog is going to have puppies does not establish when the life of a dog becomes viable. Nor does saying my daughter is pregnant indicate when my grandchild becomes a viable human being.

The last argument regarding David's belief in the concept of original sin is a very complicated discussion that would warrant an entire chapter itself. Do we all inherit the sin of Adam? Are we all sinners because Adam ate of the forbidden fruit? Is sin passed on to us from our fathers and mothers much like hair color or height? Will we discover a gene for sin?

I understand and believe in the sanctity of human life. It is truly a miracle that we exist here at all. In his book, *A Brief History of Nearly Everything*, Bill Bryson describes the unbelievable likelihood of you being on this Earth when he wrote: "If your two parents hadn't bonded just when they did—possibly to the second, possibly to the nanosecond—you wouldn't be here. And if their parents hadn't bonded in a precisely timely manner, you wouldn't be here either."

In addition, your parents had to avoid early death due to a variety of terminal illnesses and accidents, found each other mutually attractive, and decided to bond, or you wouldn't be you. The same goes for each of your grandparents, and their grandparents, and so on. It really is quite miraculous you exist in the first place and a tale of improbable survival.

I also understand that an abortion is the termination of a human life at a very early stage, directly attributed to the acts and decisions of several people.

I have personally witnessed the miracle of numerous human births, including some that have changed my life. While I am rarely at a loss for words, I cannot describe the joy that filled my heart as I watched my daughter emerge into this world. My vocabulary failed me as I watched in wonder, the very first breath of three of our perfect grandchildren. The sanctity of life is something I know and marvel.

I have studied the development of the human fetus, and understand that within weeks the zygote develops from a couple of cells into an embryo that begins to exhibit human form. I also understand that a twelve-week-old fetus is not viable outside the womb. It cannot breathe as the lungs are not fully developed and is incapable of performing the life-sustaining exchange of carbon dioxide and oxygen. Its heart has yet to develop to the point of providing the circulation necessary to survive independently. Most importantly, the brain is not fully formed nor capable of independent thought. In summary, this fetus is incapable of life independent of the mother at this point of development.

Christian theologians going all the way back to Tertullian, Origen, and even John Calvin, have denounced abortion since the early days of Christianity. The Roman Catholic Church Catechism states: "Human life must be respected and protected from the moment of conception. From the first moment of his existence, a human being must be recognized as having the rights of a person."

The Southern Baptist Convention concurs with Catholic belief by stating: "At the moment of conception, a new being enters the universe, a human being, a being created in God's image. This human being deserves our protection, whatever the circumstances of conception."

Both of these Christian denominations leave little doubt regarding the status of the earliest stages of infancy, though in practice many individual members have been known to make exceptions.

Miscarriage is relatively common for couples trying to conceive and women often experience a true sense of loss at this time. However, as a culture, we do not treat the miscarried fetus as a human infant. I am unaware of Catholics or Southern Baptists preserving the fetus by embalming, priests performing last rites, or couples having funeral services following a miscarriage. Instead the fetus is typically discarded as medical waste.

It should be pointed out that not all Christian traditions take such a rigid stance on abortion. Many denominations such as the United Church of Christ (UCC), Presbyterian Church (USA), Episcopalian Church and United Methodist Church (UMC) have taken different positions. Here is the official position as stated in *The Book of Discipline of the United Methodist Church*: "Our belief in the sanctity of unborn human life makes us reluctant to approve abortion. But we are equally bound to respect the sacredness of the life and well-being of the mother, for whom devastating damage may result from an unacceptable pregnancy."

This dogma is reflected in the motto used by the Religious Coalition for Abortion when they describe their position as "prayerfully pro-choice."

The idea of terminating a pregnancy for convenience sake, or to rectify an evening of irresponsibility, is repugnant to me. I know that it happens all too often, and as a Christian and as part of an intelligent society, I believe we should do everything possible to reduce this senseless and often selfish behavior. Christ has given us a much better example. The central theme of his ministry was to love one another, to be responsible for our actions, and to care for the disadvantaged and poor.

Many pro-choice groups also attempt to use the Bible to support their position. In addition to the quote from Genesis shown earlier, two verses are often quoted.

Genesis 2:7 *"The Lord God formed the man from the dust of the ground and breathed into his nostrils the breath of life, and man became a living being."*

This verse would appear to indicate that Adam was not man until God gave him his first breath. Much like the argument used concerning the heart by the pro-life groups, this reference indicates the basic knowledge of human anatomy at the time of this writing. Following birth, every mother anxiously awaits the reassuring first scream of her baby demonstrating the reality of the miracle of life. Conversely a commonly-used test by laymen to see if a loved one is still alive in the final stages of life is to place a hand under the nose in an effort to discern breathing. The author of Genesis clearly believes that life is found in the breath.

A second biblical reference used is found in Numbers 5:11–31. Numbers is a continuation of the dialogue between God and Moses begun in the book of Exodus and a continuation of the Mosaic Laws.

This particular reference tells how a jealous husband is to respond. God tells Moses that a husband, who believes his wife was unfaithful, is to bring barley flour to the priest as an offering. The priest then "tests" the woman by combining holy water and clay from the tabernacle floor. If the woman lies to the priest, she will be cursed and her abdomen will swell and her thigh waste away making her unable to have children. If the woman is innocent, she will not have the bitter curse and be capable of bearing children.

The pro-choice advocates believe this is an instance of God causing an abortion, therefore it cannot be a sin and equivalent to murder. Actually, the Mosaic laws command the death sentence for a variety of offenses as discussed in previous chapters. This does not appear to present a strong argument for abortion rights.

Any position regarding abortion must consider the unfortunate fact that there are people with evil intent who commit unbelievable transgressions against women. Far too many pregnancies are not the result of a reckless evening or a poor decision, but rather a vicious assault by a stranger, or even more disgusting, a relative or acquaintance.

I cannot imagine the pain and sense of violation that a woman would feel following a rape, a phenomena that has become more frequent with the introduction of date-rape drugs and excessive intoxication. The humiliation and violence of incest is most certainly a long series of personal devastations that I dare not pretend to understand. As a male, listening to detailed accounts of what many women have withstood are awful and evoke feelings of disgust and contempt.

As I consider my personal position on abortion, as a Christian father of four beautiful daughters, I have to consider the horrific scenario of any woman being forced to complete a pregnancy as a result of either of these situations. To endure the accompanying sense of guilt, shame, pain and humiliation for nine long months as her body is stretched and distorted, culminating in the unbelievable pain of childbirth would clearly exceed my definition of "cruel and unusual punishment." What is normally viewed as a necessary inconvenience to receive the incredible gift of your child conceived in love is distorted into a disgusting twenty-four-hour, seven-day-a-week, lifelong reminder of the transgression she endured. Who among us could throw the first stone in condemnation?

Although relatively rare, families are occasionally faced with life-threatening decisions regarding pregnancies. Some pregnancies create horrible decisions regarding the health of the mother or the child. As a Christian, I can't image being forced to make a decision selecting which life to save. Should my wife or daughter be faced with the awful decision of terminating a pregnancy or risking the possibility of a birth related-death, I am certain of one thing—I don't want anyone, especially the government, to make that decision for them.

We will probably never see a consolidated and unified agreement on the topic of abortion. One place to start would be agreeing that an abortion terminates the life of the fetus, and there are currently far too many abortions.

Most will agree that adoption is a wonderful option for many of these unwanted children. My personal experience attests to our ability to love our adopted children as much as biological children.

Though I disagree with the goals of the Right to Life movement, I can understand their perspective and admire their commitment. It is time we ramped back the vitriolic dialogue and eliminated terms like "baby killers" and "murderers" which are not helpful in this important discussion among faithful Christians. I believe that few of us would be willing to convict all participants with knowledge of an abortion with conspiracy to murder.

As stated at the beginning of this section, if you are looking to the Bible to support your personal view on abortion, it is simply not to be found. Even in the New Testament, when abortion was permitted under Roman law, none of the writers of the Bible choose to address the issue of abortion. Not even Paul, who wrote numerous letters to various communities concerning social and lifestyle issues, mention this volatile subject.

Stem Cell Research

As our knowledge of the human science continues to evolve, decisions involving the beginning and end of life have become more complex. This complexity opens up dialogue and conflict within the faith community.

Scientists are now able to use their God-given gifts and human minds to combat illness and extend lives. As new technologies and capabilities are discovered, the faithful will be hard pressed to find appropriate answers in the Bible.

While Jesus and the New Testament authors were aware of abortion, they chose not to address it in their biblical writings. Issues such as stem cell research, genome manipulation, organ cloning and other scientific advances not only were not addressed, they were beyond anyone's comprehension during biblical times. Now we are left to resolve these new moral challenges facing us in a faithful and Christ honoring way.

For some literalist denominations, such as Christian Scientists, the Bible has been used to deny medical treatment. While the Christian Science church says the decision to seek medical treatment is the choice of the individual, most members choose spiritual healing over conventional medicine. Founded by Mary Baker Eddy in

1866, believers use her book, *Science and Health with Key to the Scriptures*, as a companion to the Bible in much the same way as the Church of Latter Day Saints use *The Book of Mormon*.

Other more conservative denominations, like the Southern Baptists of my youth, initially condemned breakthrough medical procedures such as heart transplants and heart valve replacement using pig valves as an abomination. Rather than celebrate the new technology they instead accused doctors of "playing God." Their position was based on the biblical teaching that the heart was the center of human emotions and, more importantly, where the soul resided. They asked, how could man desecrate such a sacred part of God's creation? However, as the procedure became more popular, and members of the church embraced the concept of additional life expectancy, the position of the church was modified to accept this formerly heretical practice.

While most Christians do not follow the practice of refusing medical help, many admire those who have the conviction of following their interpretation of biblical directives. Literalists point to the book of Leviticus which is filled with remedies and treatments for skin rashes, treatment for boils, body discharges, excessive menstrual flow and even treating mildew (Leviticus 13–15). However, most Christians embrace modern healthcare especially as it pertains to their children and loved ones.

Most interpreters of sacred text are convinced they hold the secret of God's "revealed truth." One way to spread this truth is to encourage members of one denomination to attract new converts through both persuasion and procreation. Some churches go so far as to prohibit members from marrying into other faiths. Often the topic of birth control other than abstinence, female subservience to men, abortion, and suspending the prohibition of murder when it involves the killing of infidels (those of other beliefs) are examples of how church dogma can be misused.

Hidden in the serious discussion regarding stem cell research is the practice of in-vitro fertilization—the procedure of harvesting eggs from a woman and fertilizing with the sperm of the father artificially in a laboratory. Years ago the procedure was condemned by some as an effort to "play God." Gradually, however, it became more palatable for those Christian families that were unable to conceive. It is common knowledge that more eggs are taken, and fertilized, than necessary for a single birth. Many conveniently overlook the fact that the extra fertilized eggs are eventually discarded as human biological waste.

Scientists subsequently learned that stem cells in the very early stages of a fertilized egg were identical to each other and a genetic coding routed them to form a particular human organ. This led to the possibility of using these early cells to regenerate a damaged or defective adult human organ.

How incredible to dream of the possibility of regenerating a portion of a spinal column that has been severed in an accident, or of regenerating a human organ that is causing long term debilitating illness!

Overnight the discarded human waste from in-vitro clinics took on the mantle of sacred human life once scientists wanted to use them. Evangelicals immediately focused their attention on the small percentage of residual eggs that are used in stem cell research. If the eggs remain frozen and even discarded after a decade as medical waste, there is no conflict. However, if this same medical waste is being used in research to cure horrific diseases, it becomes a potential human life with all the legal protections of a child.

God has separated man from all other creatures on this Earth by giving us the intellectual ability to know right from wrong, perceive our eventual death, and the power of deduction, logic, and curiosity that enables us to unlock amazing mysteries.

Science should not be seen as the enemy of Christianity, rather the natural result of a gift from God—our incredible brains—that Christians should embrace. By celebrating these gifts we expose the true wonders of the kingdom of God.

7

Suicide: "The Unpardonable Sin"

Any discussion of social issues and the church must include suicide—a painful, yet all too common occurrence. Suicide is the second most common cause of death among American teenagers, is depressingly common among our soldiers serving in overseas conflict, and among police officers, firefighters, and other high stress occupations. In addition to those who commit suicide, another significant issue is that of assisted suicide, which has been advocated by people like Dr. Jack Kevorkian and groups such as the Hemlock Society.

While organized religion typically provides great comfort during times of sorrow, it often creates additional guilt and pain for those who survive any attempt at terminating one's life. The Catholic Church, as well as many protestant denominations, has taken a strong official position on suicide, categorizing it a "mortal sin" and declaring it the only unpardonable or unforgivable sin.

Christ never addressed the issue in the Gospels. Even Mosaic Law, which contains a total of 613 commandments, does not mention suicide. Any attempt to discover why the church finds suicide so reprehensible must begin with some basic definitions.

The Catholic Encyclopedia defines suicide as "the act of one who causes his own death, either by positively destroying his own life, as by inflicting on himself a mortal wound or injury, or by omitting to do what is necessary to escape death, as by refusing to leave a burning house."

According to this definition, the Bible mentions eight stories that involve a suicide, with all but three involving relatively minor biblical characters. Judges chapter 9 tells the story of the Israeli King Abimelech who fell on his sword to avoid being killed by a woman.

Women were considered inferior to men and to die at the hand of a woman would add insult to his death.

1 Samuel 31 and 1 Chronicles 10 tells the story of Saul falling on his sword following the death of his three sons and being seriously wounded himself. Saul first requested that his armor bearer kill him but the soldier refused. The armor bearer then fell on his own sword also. This story is repeated in 2 Samuel chapter 1, but in this version the armor bearer agrees to kill Saul. Therefore this is either a story of two suicides or of one suicide and an assisted suicide.

2 Samuel chapter 17 tells the story of Ahithophel an advisor to both King David and Absalom who became despondent that his advice was not followed and hanged himself.

In 1 Kings chapter 16 Zimri, the King of Israel, realizes that his city was being overthrown. Despondent, he went into his royal palace and set it on fire, and allowed himself to be consumed by the flames, killing himself.

The three other suicides in the Bible are more familiar to Christians. In Judges chapter 16 the great warrior Samson was said to have killed one thousand men with the jawbone of a donkey. Another more familiar story about Samson was his love for Delilah who, even after betraying him three times in an attempt to have him killed, convinced him to share the secret of his strength, which was his hair. Then in his sleep, Delilah shaved his head and betrayed him again, this time to the Philistines who captured him, gouged out his eyes, and chained him to their temple. Humiliated, he prayed to God for the strength to push over the supporting pillars, which God granted as Samson said, *"Let me die with the Philistines!"* resulting in all of their deaths, including his.

Although it is reported in only one of the gospels, Matthew 27:5, the story of the death of Judas is familiar to many. Depressed at his betrayal of Christ; Matthew reports: *"he went away and hanged himself."* This story is contradicted by the writer of the book of Acts who reports that Judas used the money from the betrayal of Jesus and *"bought a field; there he fell headlong, his body burst open and all his intestines spilled out."* Interestingly, both of these accounts are disputed in the recently discovered account of the life of Jesus, the book of Judas.

The last example of a suicide, if we use the definition provided by *The Catholic Encyclopedia*, was that of Jesus. While he certainly did not take his own life, it seems clear from all reports in the Gospels that he knew that the crowd was coming to arrest him in Gethsemane. Christ knew he would likely be crucified, yet he took no evasive action. Jesus also knew what Pilate wanted him to say in order to secure his release, yet he refused. He reportedly had the power to perform miracles but did not use this power to escape execution. These actions made his sacrifice that much more powerful. Using the definition provided by the Catholic Church—omitting to do what is necessary to escape death—then it could be argued the death of Jesus was a suicide.

One explanation for the very strong position of declaring that suicide is an "unforgivable sin" may be that the Catholic Church was afraid that their teachings made the option too attractive. If life after death was a bliss-like state, then death during a time of suffering or pain became very attractive. Paul and the Gospel writers taught that all Christians would be rewarded with a utopian image of heaven when they died. If the "heaven" they promised was so much better than life here on Earth, why would any practicing Christian want to wait?

St. Augustine of Hippo (354–386), one of the early Christian theologians, was one of the first church leaders to address the issue of suicide stating that the church must condemn it in order to survive.

The Gospel writers agreed that heaven was exclusively reserved for those of the Christian faith. While the authors disagreed on how to get to heaven or even where it was, most argued that upon death there awaits a painless and better existence. This message permeates the Christian faith. Often, upon death, comfort is provided with a phrase such as; "now he is in a better place."

For Christians who are suffering or have lost a loved one, the idea of the existence of heaven sounds attractive. Cult leaders often use this same reasoning to convince their followers to drink a poisonous drink or take fatal pills.

Fearing that the church theology may have made the concept of heaven too attractive, St. Augustine declared in his writings that suicide was a sin that could not be repented. St. Augustine believed suicide was the murder of oneself and a clear violation of the Sixth Commandment which says: "Thou shall not kill." Therefore, under Roman Catholic doctrine, all sins must be confessed and repented to a priest prior to death through the ritual of Last Rites. If someone commits suicide and is not able to confess their sins, by definition they remain unpardoned. As a result suicide carries a much higher penalty than murder since murderers are able to confess their sins to a priest following their crime.

Another early Christian writer, St. Thomas Aquinas agreed with St. Augustine and provided the following three arguments (Aquinas 1271, part II):

First: Suicide is contrary to natural self-love, whose aim is to preserve us.

I believe most of us agree that humans are born with an innate concept of self-preservation and are naturally inclined to eat and drink to sustain our life. As humans we are also instinctively aware that we should run from dangerous animals and avoid self-destructive behavior. This point sounds very logical.

However, it is equally true that some humans have a natural attraction to dangerous behaviors such as rock climbing, sky diving and other dangerous activities. It is also true that far too many self-proclaimed Christians ignore warnings that would help in achieving longer lives through such behavior as smoking, poor diet, and lack of exercise. Using this first argument, anyone who engages in dangerous lifestyles or eating habits should also be condemned should this action cause their death.

Second: Suicide injures the community of which an individual is a part.

This argument assumes that each individual has an obligation to contribute to society or, in this case, to the church. Therefore, terminating one's life prematurely hurts the remaining members. Another well-reasoned point.

However, should we also condemn someone who is terminally ill, paralyzed, or on life support? It could be argued that these individuals are no longer contributing to the community and may actually be causing a burden on the community by using communal resources.

Third: Suicide violates our duty to God because God has given us life as a gift and in taking our lives we violate his right to determine the duration of our Earthly existence.

Many Christian communities believe that our destiny is predetermined by God prior to our birth. Therefore, our life is not ours to live, but merely a role assigned to us by God for a greater good. This is also used to explain the existence of pain and suffering at the hands of an all-powerful and loving God. We experience this pain and suffering at the will of God to fulfill his greater plan that we are not able to understand.

This rule is often tossed aside by people of strong Christian faith who wish to end their suffering after a lifetime of Christian living. A common utterance of "just let me die in peace," the refusal of further medical treatment, or more active pain termination by groups like the Hemlock Society may be an exception to this rule. To many Christians, these actions are often seen as compassionate, rather than sinful.

Many of the early reformers, including Martin Luther and John Calvin, condemned suicide as strongly as the Roman Catholic Church, though both believed it was possible that God may treat the person with mercy. Luther and Calvin both challenged the Roman Catholic belief that Christ only conferred the power to forgive sins to the apostles and their successors. This coincided with their position that individual Christians could communicate directly with God. This belief allows the individual to confess sin and receive forgiveness at the time of suicide, thereby gaining a pardon directly from God.

The mainstream Protestant position on suicide could be summarized by stating that the act interferes with God's plan for one's life; is an act of self murder; and is a sin. Referencing John 3:16, Romans 10:9–13, and Ephesians 2:8–9, Protestants believe sin is forgiven the moment a person accepts Christ as savior. At that moment all past present and future sins are forgiven including the sin of suicide.

Another issue for early Christians concerned the idea of morally acceptable suicide. Augustine and Aquinas both endorsed this idea, specifically in reference to the deaths of Sampson and Jesus.

In an attempt to distinguish "morally acceptable" suicide from mortal sin, the Catholic Church created different categories of suicide deemed as acceptable to God.

Positive and direct suicides are defined as morally acceptable in certain situations. To be deemed "positive and direct," or morally acceptable, this action must have divine consent. A biblical example of a morally acceptable suicide was the death of Samson who physically destroyed the temple while praying to God that he die while killing the enemy. The church considers Samson a martyr who took his own life, along with those of 3000 Philistines, as an act of war before the executioner had an opportunity to kill him. Another example of a positive and direct suicide would be a soldier that threw himself on a grenade to save his fellow soldiers.

Morally acceptable actions that indirectly cause the death of the individual are labeled "positive" and indirect suicide. When an individual knows that his or her death is imminent, and they take no evasive action to avoid their own death, that person is said to have committed indirect suicide. An example of an indirect suicide would be a "suicide by cop." This is relatively common when a cornered criminal intentionally runs into the oncoming fire of a police force. This has been romanticized in movies like *Bonnie and Clyde* and *Butch Cassidy and the Sundance Kid.*

Indirect suicide is morally justified if a greater good is accomplished or if it has Divine consent. Jesus clearly knew that his message was a threat to both the church leaders and local authorities. After he was captured, Pilate gave him every opportunity to avoid death. Jesus, who routinely performed miracles, had the power to avoid his own death. It was, by definition, an indirect suicide. The church sees Jesus as clearly having Divine approval since his death served a greater good to all mankind.

The definition of indirect suicide is very broad and includes soldiers charging into the enemy lines in the midst of battle. During the Crusades, the pope gave "indulgences" for any crimes committed by the recruited soldiers in his army. These indulgences allowed the recipient to go directly to heaven and avoid time in purgatory required of all others. Therefore it was deemed a morally justified suicide.

Such a broad definition of indirect suicide also seems to implicate those that provide critical public services such as the death of medical personnel working with AIDS patients or other lethal diseases. The same could be argued in the case of firefighters, soldiers, and police officers who die after intentionally putting themselves in harm's way. It could be argued that their lives were shortened in pursuit of a greater good.

111

During the Enlightenment many Christians began to see significant areas of "grey" in reference to suicide and morality. In 1783 David Hume articulated this concern in his essay *On Suicide*. Hume made numerous challenges to the idea of "divine order." He maintained that since God allows us to intercede in some of God's natural order, such as diverting a river, why would he not permit us to alter his natural order for our lives? If God wants us to be happy, why would he interfere with suicide if it would relieve pain and suffering? If divine consent is required, and if God is omnipotent and sees all of our actions, doesn't that imply that God consents to all of our actions? With those arguments, Hume rejects the idea that suicide is a violation of our duty to survive at all costs. Life for those who are terminally ill or who endure unbelievable pain, it may be argued, is far worse than dying.

Hume clearly did not speak for all theologians from this era. Other noted philosophers, such as Immanuel Kant, believed suicide was an attack on our person, destroyed the very essence of our moral authority and was "debasing humanity in one's person." Kant was a strong proponent of the "sanctity of life argument" which views human life as precious and valuable in and of itself.

We often hear the sanctity of life argument used today in various situations. If life is inherently valuable and precious, it must be protected in all situations including wartime, self-defense, and capital punishment. This argument does not consider the possibility that someone who maintains a proper respect for life could reach a point of pain and suffering where they could logically make the decision to end their life. Most Christians disagree, believing that God alone has the authority to make life and death decisions.

Libertarians typically take the opposite view of suicide claiming that humans own their own bodies and therefore are morally allowed to terminate life as they wish. This argument, carried to its logical conclusion, would indicate that if we have sole ownership then no one has the moral authority to stop a suicide. This argument fails to recognize that in some situations, suicide may be harmful to others. In these situations, it could be argued, not only can we interfere with a suicide, we may have a moral obligation to do so.

Others believe suicide is moral if it is a rational decision made by a sane person and the benefit of dying far outweighs the benefit of living. This view is rejected by the Catholic Church although they recognize that insanity may be a factor in some suicides. This view has been supported by several researchers although many argue that an individual who commits suicide often acts impulsively. In these cases the individual is unable to accurately assess the severity of their own situation or the finality of the act they are about to commit.

A serious and common medical condition present in many suicides is depression. While individuals suffering from depression are not technically insane, neither are they capable of making a rational decision given their current state of mind.

Suicide nearly always causes significant pain to the survivors—leaving loved ones with questions, anger, or even guilt.

Of course, the degree of mental pain caused by a suicide differs significantly from case to case. The suicide of an elderly patient who is in tremendous pain may differ from the death of a young father and husband who seemingly had every reason to live.

Is suicide a sin?

If we define sin as an offense against God, the answer depends on your perspective of the relationship between God and man. Those that believe God has sole authority over one's life generally believe suicide is a sin. Conversely, those who believe life is a gift from God, and that man is to use this gift in a manner benefitting the will of God, might consider it a sin that may be forgiven by a loving God.

If you define sin as being any immoral act, you may be more likely to weigh the circumstances surrounding the suicide along with the mental state of the person involved before passing judgment.

There are many issues that make the topic of suicide much more complicated. Assisted suicide, soldiers returning from war committing suicide at alarmingly high rates, and our ability to artificially sustain life make the issue of suicide something we must each address on our own using the logic that God provided.

8

Religion and Oppression
of Human Rights

Slavery and Segregation

Thankfully, the practice of slavery is detested and outlawed in all civilized countries. Similarly, no Christian church or denomination would dare advocate or condone such practices. However, that was not always the case as our country was, in many ways, built on the backs of slave labor. It took the Civil War to banish slavery and the Civil Rights movement to finally put an end to overt segregation.

As for the Bible, in Leviticus God instructs the Israelites to take any *"who sojourn among you"* as slaves and they shall be *"your possessions."* In fact, it was the multitude of references to slavery throughout the inerrant Old Testament that was used extensively to justify the practice of slavery in the United States. Jefferson Davis, the President of the Confederate States stated this position quite clearly when he declared that slavery: "was established by decree of Almighty God... it is sanctioned in the Bible, in both Testaments, from Genesis to Revelation... it has existed in all ages, has been found among the people of the highest civilization, and in nations of the highest proficiency in the arts."

Davis was only one of many politicians that used the Bible as justification for the practice of slavery and segregation. For those that believe in the inferiority of people of color, the Bible provides numerous veiled references to justify this immorality. The power of this message, when delivered from a church pulpit, can be powerful.

During the Civil War, reports from the prison camps raised serious concerns to President Lincoln. In one of his letters he voiced concern that the commitment of the Confederate soldiers was greater than the Union soldiers as they appear to be praying more vigorously.

Some writers, in attempting to reconcile the numerous biblical references to slavery, point out that slavery in the Bible was different than that in the United States as it was not based on skin color. That is true; skin color was not a major factor since anyone who was not an Israelite was a potential slave.

Some also claim that biblical slavery was actually more like a hired hand or employee and the work conditions were not bad. Actually, Leviticus 25:39 provides a clear differentiation between a hired worker and a slave when it states: *"If one of your countrymen becomes poor among you and sells himself to you, do not make him work as a slave. He is to be treated as a hired worker or a temporary resident among you."*

It goes on to differentiate by saying, *"Do not rule over them ruthlessly."*

In fact, it wasn't just slavery that southern Christians used the Bible to justify; they also used it to support their hatred for blacks through the expression of racism and segregation.

Even today there remain websites supporting the concept that God ordained that the races be kept apart so that the purity of the white race is kept intact. These fringe websites teach that the greatest form of genocide would be to allow the mixture with the black or yellow race. The term they use is the same term that was used in many churches in reference to interracial dating and marriages: "mongrelization." Quotes from Leviticus, Exodus, Psalms and Hosea are used to support this ridiculous claim.

Does it seem ironic that these same people believe that Christ, who was most likely a dark skinned Jew, was worried about the purity of the Caucasian race?

They continue with a quote from Deuteronomy 7:3: *"Do not intermarry with them. Do not give your daughters to their sons or take their daughters for your sons."*

This sounds very convincing. But, who is "them?" It turns out that this is God's direction to the Israelites to destroy their enemies when they enter a new territory. God commands that they must *"destroy them totally."* The "them" he is talking about in verse 3 are listed in verse 1 as the Hittites, Girgashites, Amorites, Canaanites, Perizzites, Hivites, and Jebusites. It is basically everyone that is not an Israelite and has nothing to do with race.

For years many fundamentalist pastors have spewed this hatred from the pulpit. Thankfully most will not tolerate it today. It is not what Jesus taught nor is it the message of a loving Christ who spent his time in the company of social outcasts and those who were downtrodden.

Those who quote Leviticus and Deuteronomy for guidance from God seem to ignore the message found in Matthew 27:50–51: *"And when Jesus had cried out again in a loud voice, he gave up his spirit. At that moment the curtain of the temple was torn in two from top to bottom."*

I was taught that the tearing of the curtain was the symbol that Mosaic Law was no longer valid. As a result people did not need to sacrifice burnt offerings to God, as instructed in Exodus and Leviticus, and individuals were allowed to speak directly to God in prayer. We were informed that the need for offerings and the teachings of the Mosaic Laws were obsolete. Christ came to Earth to provide a new set of laws.

Christ taught us to love our enemies, give to the needy with modesty, to pray quietly and not to judge others. In Matthew 5:3–11, the verses referred to as the Beatitudes, we are told: *"blessed are the poor, those who mourn, the meek, those who hunger, the merciful, the pure of heart, the peacemakers and the persecuted."*

Christ didn't teach us to separate ourselves from those that are not like us. He taught us to seek them out.

Christ teaches us in Matthew 7:15; *"Watch out for the false prophets. They come to you in sheep's clothing, but inwardly they are ferocious wolves. By their fruit you will recognize them."*

True messengers for Christ do not distort his teachings. It is not the color of your skin that makes you Christ-like, but rather how you live your life, what you say, and what you think. When Christ was providing an explanation for not fasting he gave us a wonderful lesson in appearances: Matthew 15:11 *"What goes into a man's mouth does not make him unclean, but what comes out of his mouth, that is what makes him unclean."*

The real message of Christ is that of tolerance. While Paul was not tolerant of the depravity of the Romans and Greeks, he did teach tolerance when he proclaimed: Galatians 3:28 *"There is neither Jew nor Greek, slave nor free, male nor female, for you are all one in Christ Jesus."*

The voice that speaks to us in our quietest moments tells us that it is wrong to practice intolerance. It is time that we listen to the God that is within us.

The Role of Women in the Church

As in other areas of our society, one of the most dramatic changes in the church over the past twenty years involves the role of women. Until a few years ago many denominations did not allow female pastors or elders, instead relegating them to Sunday school teachers or non-decision-making roles. Slowly that has been changing even though a glass ceiling still exists in many of the more conservative church traditions. To break the gender barrier, the church and its leaders have had to overcome many scriptural references that were not exactly female friendly.

The Bible teaches the subservient role of women all the way back to the creation story. For example, Paul's perspective on the role of women in 1 Timothy 2:11: *"A woman should learn in quietness and full submission. I do not permit a woman to teach or to have authority over a man; she must be silent. For Adam was formed first, then Eve. And Adam was not the one deceived; it was the woman who was deceived and became the sinner. But woman will be saved through childbearing—if they continue in faith, love, and holiness with propriety."*

In the Old Testament daughters often suffered the wrath of God, as mentioned earlier with the story of Sodom. If fact, if one was in need of money, according to Exodus 21:7–11, it was within a father's right to sell his daughter into slavery.

Women are clearly taking a more prominent role in society, as well as in most Christian churches as they teach Sunday school, become ordained ministers, are elected elders, and assume supervisory positions within the church.

It's interesting to note that those who believe in an inerrant Bible are slowly coming around to accepting societal norms.

There are still challenges. Few if any of the largest mega churches have yet to call a female pastor. Many of the most progressive churches struggle with hiring women pastors even though many of the leading theological schools graduate more women than men.

PART THREE
The Church: Past, Present, and Future

We have looked into the history of the Bible, how the Christian church has interpreted it to foster its agenda, and current beliefs of many Americans. In this section we find ways progressives can find a way forward while holding onto their beliefs.

9

A Short History of the Church

For many decades, major polling organizations like Gallup, The Pew Forum on Religion and Public Life and ARIS (American Religious Identification Survey) have been asking Americans about their affiliations and beliefs when it comes to the church and religion. In the past decade the overwhelming evidence points to a growing number of individuals who are no longer involved in any religious organization.

In the last ten years the percentage of those no longer affiliated with any religion has nearly doubled from just over eight percent to fifteen percent (ARIS 2008). Much of this dramatic change can be attributed to the growing wariness people have with organized religion. Today, according to Gallup, around forty percent of individuals regularly attend church in spite of over seventy-six percent (down from eighty-five percent two decades ago) saying they are Christian. Somewhere there is a disconnect between saying one is part of a religious community and actually showing up. Some denominational research says that a third of Americans are fully involved in a church with another third only occasionally showing up for worship leaving the remaining third having no faith involvement at all.

To gain a better understanding of how this happened requires us to look into the history of the Christian church from its early days after biblical times to its growth as a major worldwide religion.

Building a Religion

The Christian church has a checkered history.

After the end of Christ's ministry on Earth, those following the teachings of Jesus were a small and disorganized group. Those remaining pretty much had to build their own belief system and organization from the ground up, with one eye toward the ministry of Jesus and the other on how to spread his message.

Then, during the reign of Constantine (306–337 AD) as Roman emperor, the unimaginable happened. Constantine himself, the most powerful man on Earth, converted from sun worshiper to the Christian faith. Not only did he experience a conversion experience, he also declared the Roman Empire a Christian theocracy.

In order to bring organization and a single theology to this huge new group of potential converts, Constantine convened a meeting of the leading bishops and theologians in order to bring all Christians together under one doctrinal rule. The council, which met during the year 325 in the city of Nicaea, was told to determine which writings belonged together in one volume and which did not. What resulted was the first Christian Bible. Also established was a hierarchy to rule the newly organized religion and a single creed that all would be forced to adopt in order to be a member of this new faith.

That document is known today as the Nicene Creed, which has itself been refined and edited through the centuries. Below is the version from the year 381 and still used by many churches today:

We believe in one God,
The Father, the Almighty,
Of all that is, seen and unseen.

We believe in one Lord, Jesus Christ
the only Son of God,
eternally begotten of the Father,
God from God, Light from Light,
true God from true God begotten, not made,
of one Being with the Father.
Through him all things were made.
For us and for our salvation
He came down from heaven:
by the power of the Holy Spirit

He became incarnate from the Virgin Mary,
and was made man.
For our sake he was crucified under Pontius Pilate;
He suffered death and was buried.
On the third day he rose again
in accordance with the Scriptures;
He ascended into heaven
and is seated at the right hand of the Father.
He will come again in glory to judge the living and the dead,
and his kingdom will have no end.

We believe in the Holy Spirit, the Lord, the giver of life,
who proceeds from the Father and the Son.
With the Father and the Son he is worshipped and glorified.
He has spoken through the Prophets.
We believe in one holy catholic and apostolic Church.
We acknowledge one baptism for the forgiveness of sins.
We look for the resurrection of the dead,
and the life of the world to come. Amen.

The Nicene Creed is often used to determine who is "in" and who is "out" when it comes to the Christian faith. In the centuries prior to the founding of the United States, most countries had state-sponsored religion. In fact, that was one of the primary reasons the early settlers left their countries to come to the new world.

In state sponsored religion the Nicene Creed was often used to determine if someone was a true Christian. If a person refused to re-cite the Creed they risked being tried for heresy, which, if convicted, could result in a long prison sentence, torture or even execution.

Today, countries with state-sponsored churches rarely, if ever, insist on members making a public pronouncement of their Christian faith. However, that is not the case in many Muslim countries where Islamic Law or Sharia is not only sacred—someone violating it is prosecuted in much the same way as in early Christian countries.

The wisdom of our founding fathers to prohibit a national religion is never more clearly appreciated than when we examine the countries that currently have an official state religion.

To put this in perspective, after the reign of Constantine the Roman Catholic Church became more influential. As with most power there is a tendency for it to corrupt and even bring on paranoia. In the case of the early Catholic Church many of its ruling bishops decided to take a more aggressive approach to any perceived challenge to its authority by punishing those it saw as disagreeing with its decrees and persecuting them as a nonbelievers or heretics.

One theologian that disagreed with the actions of early church leaders was Tertullian from Carthage, in the Roman province of Africa. Tertullian wrote prolifically during the second century prior to the time of Constantine and believed the acceptance of Christianity was a matter of free will and should not be forced on anyone. In his writings Tertullian opposed the branding of nonbelievers as heretics. His beliefs eventually caused him to split from the Christian church; though today his writings have been accepted by the church.

Tertullian along with two prominent voices of the early church, Origen and Lactantius, explained that the laws given by God to Moses were no longer applicable as Jesus provided a new standard for all Christians. They took the position that denounced killing and torture as appropriate punishment for heretics.

However, the writings of scholars like Tertullian were not followed by many in the church. Instead, the church continued the practice of punishing those accused of being a heretic often leading to the church confiscating the property of the offender. This accomplished two objectives; it eliminated the accused from speaking publicly and filled the church coffers.

The efforts of the early church to have everyone accept official church doctrine went much further. After Constantine, with the power of the Roman government behind it, the church was able to wage war against heretics in increasingly bitter and savage ways. These escalated into some of the most sadistic and barbaric acts ever committed against humanity—all in the name of Christ.

As the Church continued to grow during the fourth century, it also began to divide among the churches of Eastern Europe, primarily based in Constantinople, and the Roman Church based in Europe. This East-West Schism, as it came to be called, was a result of many doctrinal, geographical, and theological differences. Ultimately Christianity divided into the Roman Catholic Church and the Eastern Orthodox Church.

Later, during the seventh century, the Prophet Mohammad formed Islam which began to spread throughout the Middle East. This set the stage for even more conflict between the various religions, which continues to this day.

The Crusades

Within 800 years after the crucifixion of Jesus, Judaism, the Eastern and Western branches of Christianity, and Islam were each making claim to God's truth.

In addition, local kingdoms, possessing large, well-trained armies, began to expand their territories. This resulted in battles between adjacent Christian kingdoms for supremacy. Finally, the Roman Catholic Church decided to intercede to stop the local wars between Christians by unifying them in crusades against two common enemies: followers of Islam and Judaism.

Pope Alexander II gave his blessing to the Christians fighting against the Muslims in the Iberian Peninsula by providing an indulgence to any soldier killed in battle. The indulgence promised that any soldier killed in battle would avoid purgatory and go straight to heaven.

This granting of indulgences became a great recruiting tool. It's similar to what some young Muslims are promised today—the company of seventy-two virgins—if they strap on a suicide vest and kill innocents.

The pope also presented the soldiers with a cross which was part of their uniform—making them soldiers of the Church—readying them to fight, kill, rape, and plunder in the name of God. Soldiers felt invincible while wearing the cross from the church having been provided with the promise of direct invitation to heaven upon their death whether a sinner or not. The remission of sin turned out to be a tremendous recruitment tool and continued to be offered for the next couple centuries, from 1095 until the early 1300s, as the Crusades dragged on.

Armed with the promise of a direct path to heaven from the pope, these soldiers' vengefulness led to the systemic slaughter of innocents at the hands of famous Crusaders like Richard I (Richard the Lionheart) who would sign treaties with small villages while promising safe harbor for its citizens before ordering his army to massacre them. Richard justified his actions because he felt treaties with non-Christians were not valid, a similar argument made by radical Muslims today.

Crusaders showed no mercy as they systemically slaughtered all Jews they encountered by raping, murdering, and pillaging city after city all while wearing the cross of Christ and the promise of forgiveness by the pope.

It is often argued that the Crusades were critical in preserving the Roman Catholic Church and quashing the threat of Judaism and Islam. It is thought much of the wealth of today's Church—land, art, buildings—can still be attributed to the Crusades.

The Inquisition

In 1231—sixty years prior to the date most historians agree marks the end of over two hundred years of Crusades—Pope Gregory IX instituted a judicial procedure in order to seek out and then try those the Church considered heretics. This is now referred to as The Inquisition and the idea was to "make inquisition" of those who were thought to have committed heresy. The Church defined a heretic as anyone who held beliefs that conflicted with its official dogma.

Whenever someone was suspected of being a heretic an "inquisitor" was sent to investigate. Most inquisitors were friars from Dominican or Franciscan orders who worked in cooperation with local bishops. Together they would hold a town meeting where they would ask if any of those in attendance knew of someone who had committed heresy. When someone made an accusation, the accused could either admit to heresy or deny it. For those who admitted to the charges, they would be forgiven and sent back to their family. However, those who did not repent were held for trial, and if convicted, were either imprisoned or executed.

Later, in 1252, Pope Innocent IV upped the ante by authorizing torture to be used as a way to gain confessions. The reason was because many bishops were not very successful at eradicating heretical groups from their regions. Over the next hundred years the Vatican developed standards and trained groups of "inquisitors" to more effectively find and punish heretics.

It is hard to imagine living during the time of the inquisitions and having the Church taking away personal freedom. This is not unlike what is happening today in much of the Muslim world where women can be stoned to death just for being accused of being unfaithful to their spouse.

The biblical justification given by the Church in sanctioning inquisitions is found in the parable of the Vine and the Branches.

John 15:1–3 *"I am the true vine, and my Father is the gardener. He cuts off every branch in me that bears no fruit, while every branch that does bear fruit he prunes so that it will be even more fruitful."*

John 15: 6 *"If anyone does not remain in me, he is like a branch that is thrown away and withers; such branches are picked up, thrown into the fire and burned."*

It fostered the idea of Papal infallibility by declaring the pope "father" just as Jesus states that "my father" is the gardener. Papal infallibility is a very integral part of Catholic theology stating that by the power of the Holy Spirit, the pope is without error in matters regarding faith or morals when derived from divine revelation.

It also exposes the issue of taking a few verses out of context. The message from John 15 goes on to say: John 15:11–13 *"I have told you this so that my joy may be in you and that your joy may be complete. My command is this: Love each other as I have loved you. Greater love has no one than this, that he lay down his life for his friends."*

To reinforce his intended lesson from the parable, John states in verse 17: *"This is my command: Love each other."*

The pope instead chose to take a single phrase from this parable about loving one another to justify inflicting a horrific and painful death upon anyone who dared disagree with him.

Inquisitors did not wait for individuals to speak out openly against those they suspected of violating the teachings of the church. One could also make an accusation in private to the inquisitor. For example, if someone did not like their neighbor, they could anonymously make an unfounded charge of heresy to the inquisitor. This resulted in the accused being arrested, brought before an inquisitor and charged with heresy. The accused was never allowed to confront the accuser and was assumed guilty. Only if the accused confessed was there any chance for forgiveness and escaping torture.

By denying the charges the accused was assumed to be resisting, resulting in the use of many hideous methods of torture to elicit a confession. This meant the individual would be tortured ruthlessly in one room then brought before the inquisitor to confess. If the confessor recanted the story told under torture, he had proven himself to be a liar, and returned for more torture. Torturers were permitted as much time as required to elicit a confession and allow the accused to give names of others who could be brought up on charges. It wasn't enough to simply enter a "guilty" plea. This increased the number of people being turned over to the authorities for heresy.

Torture itself was not considered a punishment; it was simply a method for extracting the "truth." Punishment followed.

There were rules for torture. It could not cause the loss of life or limb, nor provoke bleeding. These restrictions forced the inquisitors to be creative in the methods and devices used in extracting confessions.

"The Brodequin" was a box that was strapped to the ankles and feet containing a large screw device that was tightened by hand until the ankles and feet were crushed. This obviously complied with the rules as the victim lived, and even though the feet were useless, no blood was shed.

The "Stappado" used a rope suspended from the ceiling as the victims hands were tied behind the back and raised to the ceiling dislocating both shoulders simultaneously. To increase the pain, weights would be attached to the ankles to insure most joints in the body would be dislodged.

The "Rack" was a device that attached ropes to the arms and legs which was used to gradually pull the victims arms and legs in opposite directions. If the victim lost consciousness, they were revived, and it was assumed that they were faking to resist confession. After regaining consciousness, the torture would become more aggressive.

Later, the use of the "Judas Cradle" became popular. This was a large wooden spike over which the naked victim was suspended by ropes from the ceiling. The torture was performed by repeatedly lowering the victim onto the spike piercing the body in multiple areas. Church documents also inform us that the skin of the victim could be stripped down to the waist without immediate death.

All of these methods of torture were approved, sanctioned, and carried out by the inquisitors who were appointed by the pope in the name of Jesus.

During the Inquisition thousands were executed for heresy. Most of those accused confessed and judgment was handed down. Typically the repentant heretic would face anything from a requirement to do good deeds, such as building churches or roads; be sent on a pilgrimage, sometimes for years; or required to wear a colored cross stitched into their clothing. More extreme punishment included being whipped with rods and the confiscation of all property.

Those that professed a belief other than official Church dogma were sentenced to anything from excommunication to being burned at the stake in a process called "Auto da fe" or translated, "Act of Faith." During this Sunday ceremony the heretic was walked through the courtyard wearing a "san benito," which was a tunic upon which was painted a likeness of the victim burning in flames with depictions of dragons and devils. This indicated to the crowd that the victim would be burned alive. If the san benito was decorated with the flames pointing downward, the victim would be strangled prior to being burned at the stake, and a painted cross indicated that the heretic's life would be saved and he would be forced to do penance.

The family of the heretic would not be spared as they would be forced to pay for the expenses of the trial and forfeit all property and land to the church.

Joan of Arc is a well-known example of a victim of the inquisitions. Despite her illiteracy, she impressed generations by defending herself courageously and intelligently during her trial.

In an attempt to gain an admission of heresy, Joan was asked if "she knew she was in God's grace?" Realizing it was a trap she measured her words carefully since church dogma stated that no one could be certain of being in God's grace. If she said "no," she would be confessing her guilt, if she said "yes," that would prove she was heretic. Joan answered; "If I am not, may God put me there; and if I am, may God so keep me." In spite of her devotion to the church, she was convicted and burned at the stake. Her ashes were shown to the public to prove she did not escape, and burned twice more to make certain that nothing remained. Years later, following her execution, she was declared a martyr by the church.

While these awful practices are disturbing, the explanation still provided by sources today—such as that in *The Catholic Encyclopedia*—are unacceptable. Though the church acknowledges that prior to the year 1220, some individuals made mistakes, the Church has never accepted guilt or asked for forgiveness. Instead the inquisition is brushed aside stating: "the occasional executions of heretics during this period must be ascribed partly to the arbitrary action of individual rulers, partly to the fanatic outbreaks of overzealous populace, and in no way to ecclesiastical law."

In other words, despite the fact that thousands were executed under the pope's direct orders and that an entire judicial system was established to carry out these mockeries of justice, it was actually not the fault of the church—it was merely the solo acts of "arbitrary individuals."

From the Church's perspective, what made the inquisition truly unique was that the pope established permanent judges to deal legally with the offenders. Instead of it being a black mark on Christianity, some have re-spun history as a triumphant time that should be celebrated.

The Reformation

Part of what made the Church so powerful was the inability of lay Christians to gain access to the written Bible. This changed when Christians, such as English lay minister John Wycliffe, translated

133

the Bible into English. Wycliffe was one of the first in a long line of dissenters to successfully challenge the Roman Catholic Church in what was to become the Protestant movement.

Also part of the movement was Jan Huss, a Czech priest from Bohemia who was rector of the Czech University. Huss, like Wycliffe, became increasingly dissatisfied with the teachings of the Church. His "Hussian" movement began to create a serious separation from the church in Rome. Huss taught that the Church should be banned from creating rules that were not biblical. He went on to declare disagreement with the Crusades, and that a pope or bishop did not have the authority to take up the sword in the name of the Church. Huss also agreed with Wycliffe in his opposition to the practice of selling indulgences.

In response, during the 1414 General Council of the Church, which had convened in the Germanic city of Constance, Emperor Sigismund of Luxemburg tried to mediate the enormous schism that had grown between the Hussians and Rome. The Emperor convinced Huss to attend with a promise of guaranteeing his safety. But, instead, Huss was arrested shortly after his arrival angering Emperor Sigismund. To convince the Emperor, the bishops said Huss would be given the chance to explain himself in court. However Huss refused to recant his beliefs and was subsequently burned at the stake. His last words were reported to be: "in a hundred years, God will raise up a man whose calls for reform cannot be suppressed."

As prophesied, in 1517—102 years later—Martin Luther, a German priest and theology professor, posted his dissertation titled *Ninety-Five Theses of Contention* on the door of the Cathedral. This sparked the beginning of the Protestant Reformation. In his theses, Luther—who drew strongly from the writings of Huss and Wycliffe—criticized numerous Church practices and doctrines as unbiblical.

Unlike Huss and Wycliffe before him, Luther's writings were easily disseminated throughout Europe due to the invention of the printing press, invented in 1440 by Johannes Gutenberg. An initial printing of two hundred copies of the Bible was available in 1455, and thousands of copies were in print by Luther's time. While the Church could easily suppress the Hussians by collecting and destroying their writings—since all were copied by hand resulting in very few copies—the printing press allowed the message of Luther to spread quickly.

Luther's message differed from Roman Catholic dogma in four primary areas:

1. Salvation is gained through faith alone and faith is a free gift from God. No amount of prayer, confession, good deeds, or money paid to the church could affect one's salvation.

2. Communication with God is open to all believers and does not require an intermediary from the Church. Therefore members of the clergy nor church leaders have an elevated status in the eyes of God.

3. God's Word is only found in the Bible, which is God's revealed truth.

4. All people serve God, not just those in the priesthood.

The most significant concepts introduced by Luther were that all people could communicate with God without the intercession by a priest and that the practice of indulgences were wrong. This essentially eliminated the concept of the infallible pope.

Soon, the Lutheran movement in Germany drew significant attention in England, which motivated an Oxford scholar named William Tyndale to complete the first English language version of the New Testament from the original Greek. The Church quickly labeled the books as heretic and demanded all copies be burned. But rather than resulting in the eradication of the English language Bible, it actually increased its exposure which helped finance a second printing.

The Tyndale Bible soon spread throughout England giving rise to numerous Protestant movements. One movement, which the Church labeled as Anabaptists, professed the abolition of tithing to the state-sanctioned Church and refusal to enter military service. This introduced the concept of separation of Church and State. These so-called Anabaptists also believed in only baptizing adults who were old enough to provide their "consent." The name Anabaptist, which stood for "re-baptizer," was used by the Church in a derogatory manner, to signify the practice of baptizing those who were previously baptized by the Catholic Church at infancy.

In 1529 the Assembly of the Holy Roman Empire met, which is referred to as the Diet of Speyer, because the meeting took place in the German city of Speyer. The Assembly made two significant declarations: It labeled the followers of Luther as Protestants for the first time and it proclaimed the death penalty for the act of re-baptizing.

The Church essentially went to war against both the Protestants and anyone that dared to translate or read from the Holy Bible. Despite this, William Tyndale, along with his friend John Frith, continued to translate the books of the New Testament along with the first five books of the Old Testament. For their efforts both Tyndale and Frith were tried by the court, convicted of heresy and burned at the stake.

For a short time, during the reign of Edward VI in England, Protestantism was made legal resulting in a break from Rome. However, when his daughter, Mary, succeeded him as queen she restored Catholicism in England. This resulted in the burning of over 300 Protestants including over 100 priests and bishops starting with an associate of Tyndale, John Rogers.

In spite of the best efforts of the Roman Catholic Church, Protestantism had taken a foothold in Europe and was spreading rapidly. Not only was the Church unsuccessful in suppressing these new denominations, their actions led some to find another home to practice their faith.

10

The Church Expands to America

In spite of persecution, the growth of Protestantism continued throughout Europe. While the substantive differences between most Protestant denominations and the Catholic Church seem somewhat insignificant today, they directly led to the migration to the New World by Christians in search of religious freedom. Beginning in 1620, with the arrival of the Pilgrims and the establishment of the Plymouth Colony in present day Massachusetts, it could be argued that the settlement of America was directly the result of the many battles between Protestants and the Roman Catholic Church.

The Salem Witch Trials

Starting with the arrival of the Pilgrims, America soon became home to people from many Protestant groups including Quakers, Anabaptists and Puritans. While they initially lived in relative harmony, by the late 1600s several events conspired to cause division. Because the New World's economy was primarily based on agriculture, it was to a family's benefit to have many children in order to insure enough workers. But the next generation required even more land in which to survive. To make matters worse, blights were common and could easily wipe out a year's crop. This prompted families to move further into the wilderness to find more land resulting in an encroachment into Native lands.

Because the mostly Pilgrim population believed all losses were the result of the wrath of God, increasingly it was thought there were people within their own community who were responsible for the divine judgment they were receiving.

Then came the trigger that led to one of the worst religious chapters in the new country's history.

Cotton Mather, the minister of Boston's North Church, and a believer in witchcraft began to describe the behavior of the four children of local mason John Goodwin as being strange. He attributed their behavior to the influence of the Goodwin Irish housekeeper, Ann Glover, who practiced witchcraft. This resulted in her trial and execution in 1689.

By 1692, the practice of witchcraft was at a fever pitch resulting in hundreds of accusations, scores of trials and dozens executed. Finally, in 1693, those remaining in prison were released because their arrests were found to be baseless.

The witch trials are an example of how the values and morals the pilgrims brought over to the New World could erupt into mob attacks on innocents.

While the church typically did not perform the witch trials, the strong church-state association that was prevalent at that time—and still continues throughout the world today with other religions—are clearly an affront to a civilized world.

The Salem Witchcraft Trials were an aftermath of a world that had recently survived the bubonic plague and people were looking for a villain that would perpetrate such a hideous torture on children and entire families. The practice of medicine was extremely crude prior to the twentieth century and there was little knowledge of bacteria and viruses. This was before the age of modern science and, as a result, church leaders consulted with the Bible for answers.

The Bible taught that the reason for plague and disease was the work of sorcery and witches. Deuteronomy 18:11–12 calls anyone who practices sorcery as, *"detestable to the Lord,"* while Exodus 22:18 says, *"do not allow a sorceress to live."* To early settlers, if sorcery caused disease, and if God hated sorcery, then it made sense that all witches must die.

The Church and Slavery

Slavery was a part of the history of America from the time the first settlers arrived in Jamestown in 1619 when a Dutch ship brought twenty enslaved Africans to the first colony in the New World. The slave trade continued to be legal until 1808 and continued underground until the dawn of the Civil War in 1861. During that time millions of Africans were grabbed from their homes and transported to the New World against their will. At its height, the slave population in the United States grew to over three million.

The church justified the concept of slavery using biblical verses based on Genesis 9:25–27: *"Cursed by Canaan! The lowest of slaves will he be to his brothers."* And continues: *"Blessed be the Lord, the God of Shem! May Canaan be the slave of Shem. May God extend the territory of Japheth; may Japeth live in the tents of Shem and may Canaan be his slave."*

While the white churches found biblical justifications in holding slaves, at the same time the slaves in the south and free blacks in the north were themselves forming churches. The first black churches were formed prior to 1800 by free blacks in the northern United States. At the same time slaves were starting their own churches. However, following a slave revolt in the early 1800s the Commonwealth of Virginia passed a law which required that black churches have white pastors.

After the Civil War the proud tradition of the African-American church has continued through the establishment of denominations that still thrive today. These include the Church of God in Christ (COGIC), African Methodist Episcopal Church (AME), African Methodist Episcopal Zion Church (AME Zion), and many independent churches. These denominations were the foundation for the Civil Rights movement of the 1960s and continue to be a great influence on the African American community.

The Church and Racism

Racism has been and continues to be a shameful part of our American life and, unfortunately, Christianity.

The race riots of the 1960s were a rude awakening to our nation, myself included. I had been taught in school that the Confederate states tried to secede from the Union over the issue of slavery which ended with Lincoln's *Emancipation Proclamation*.

My Christian education on the issue of race began at a very early age as we sang:

Jesus loves the little children, all the children of the world.
Red and yellow, black and white,
they are precious in his sight,
Jesus loves the little children of the world.

This was typically part of our education regarding the story of the Tower of Babel from chapter 11 of Genesis. The story takes place a couple hundred years after the Great Flood when God killed all mankind except for the righteous Noah and his family. Genesis tells us that all of the people of the world lived in one city, Shinar, and spoke one language. In Genesis 11:4 the people tried building a tower that: *"reaches to the heavens, so that we may make a name for ourselves and not be scattered over the face of the whole earth."*

In verse 6 God responds saying: *"If as one people speaking the same language they have begun to do this then nothing they plan to do will be impossible for them."*

God then scattered the people over the face of the Earth.

This story provides the biblical explanantion of why people are dispersed around the globe and speak different languages. It can also provide a justification for racism and segregation.

In my fundamental Baptist upbringing I was repeatedly taught that the lesson of Babel is that God does not want the races intermingling. He intentionally placed the blacks in Africa, the whites in Europe, the reds (Native Americans) in America, and the yellows

(Asians) in Asia. We were told that efforts to integrate our neighbor-hoods and schools were an attempt to defy the will of God.

This prompted me to ask to our pastor, "If God wanted the races separated, isn't it the fault of the pilgrims since they came to an America designated for the red race? How about the white slave traders who kidnapped and transported the blacks to America?"

My pastor explained that the whites are God's chosen race who claim dominion over all other races.

The idea of the white race being chosen by God formed the cornerstone of many American Christian denominations to justify slavery and segregation. It was openly taught in some schools and churches into the late 1960s and still can be found on many Internet websites today.

While it is difficult to understand today, the theology of the supe-riority of the white race was clearly one of the underlying premises of much of the racism that founded this country. Though rarely taught in churches today, far too many whites profess this belief in private conversations or through crude jokes or comments.

The idea of white superiority was justified in Christian communi-ties by cleverly manipulating two stories from the book of Genesis.

The first doctrine is referred to as the "Curse of Ham," and is found in Genesis chapter 9. Following the Great Flood, Noah became intoxicated and fell into a deep sleep naked and uncovered in his tent. His youngest son, Ham, discovered him lying there and instead of covering his nakedness, he went to get his brothers. Without ac-tually looking at Noah the brothers covered him up while turning their heads to avoid gazing at his nakedness.

When Noah awoke and heard that his youngest son had seen him naked in his drunken slumber, he cursed Ham saying: *"Cursed be Canaan! The lowest of slaves will he be to his brothers."*

Using this simple story of an angry drunken Noah yelling at his son for his own transgression, some in the Christian community added to the story by declaring, without any evidence, that the sons of Ham were the settlers of Africa. Therefore, in this elaborate contortion of the facts, they determined that blacks were cursed by Noah, and therefore by God, to be slaves.

The second biblical doctrine used to justify the argument that God ordained superiority to the Caucasian race is referred to as the "Serpent Seed Doctrine." This doctrine teaches that the temptation of Eve was actually sexual, and she was ultimately raped by Satan, which produced a "half-breed" child, Cain. The proponents of this doctrine point out that Genesis 4:15 states that God placed a "mark" on Cain so everyone could avoid these people. They then claim, erroneously, that the name Adam means "the man who blushes." Therefore, the mark placed on all sons of Satan is the inability to blush. Although I have personally witnessed blushing by those in all races, the proponents of this doctrine offer this as proof that non-European Caucasians are the half-breed descendants of Satan. Following the Civil War, as movements to suppress the rights of blacks were raging, a Nashville minister, Buckner H. Payne, went so far as to claim that the tempter of Eve was Satan in the form of a black man.

Most who believe in the superiority of the white race have not developed such a complicated explanation to justify their belief. It is clear that throughout our nation's history, the Christian Bible was used as the underlying premise to support our mistreatment of people of color.

In spite of this often subtle but repeated indoctrination, and living in an all white rural community, I never thought of myself as racist. My first year of college was truly an eye-opening experience as I attempted to win a basketball scholarship at a small Division II school. I was assigned to share a room with two black athletes and was across the hall from the first Jew that I ever met.

It can be a bit intimidating to share a room with strangers. I was doubly apprehensive, yet excited, for the opportunity to be exposed to a new culture. My new roommates were very helpful and immediately attempted to make me feel comfortable by introducing me to their predominately black friends. The experience made me feel certain I had transcended racism.

One evening seven of us were sitting in the living room of our small dorm when the discussion turned to racism. I explained to them that I was not raised to be a racist in spite of my rural, conservative, Christian upbringing. To this day, I can still recall my new roommate Bobby looking me directly in the eye and saying, "I believe you, but do me a favor and finish this sentence. Eenie, meenie, miney moe..."

That was a phrase I had used countless times as a child in selecting teammates for a game of pickup baseball, football, or basketball. We now complete the rhyme with "catch a tiger by the toe." However the rhyme I was taught and repeated so innocently for my entire early life ended with "catch a nigger by the toe."

This was during a time of incredible gains on the part of the civil rights movement and only a couple of years after the terrible race riots of the late 1960s. Until that moment it never occurred to me how ingrained racial slurs had formed my education, my Christian faith, and my life.

Out of embarrassment, I hung my head and shook it side to side in utter silence. When I looked up, Bobby and his friends were staring at me in anticipation of my response. I quietly responded: "Apparently, I have a lot to learn."

That was 1971, and in the interim, with the help of some wonderful classes in black history and forming friendships with several friends of color, I have learned a lot.

Unfortunately, racism is still a very big part of our lives. I have been incredibly blessed with a successful business that has allowed my wife Irene and me to experience nearly every state in this great nation and meet some truly extraordinary people. Unfortunately, it has also shown us that racism is not limited to the poor and uneducated. In private conversations, and unsolicited e-mails sent to select groups, it is clear that many Americans still harbor some of the ignorant prejudices that I experienced back in the 1970s. It is much more subtle now, but it is still there. Far too often, those revealing this bigotry are pillars in their communities and churches.

The public education is another source of racism I received while growing up. Back then they were very careful to omit the racist nature of our national heritage and manipulate our history to "protect" us from the truth of our past. Students of African American studies are quick to point out the pro-slavery slant used in our textbooks. James W. Loewen summarized and documented this systemic misinformation in his book *Lies My Teacher Told Me.*

Racism in America can be traced all the way back to the voyages of Christopher Columbus who, during his first excursion to the New World kidnapped six native Arawak people and transported them back to Spain to either convert to Christianity or for use as servants. By this time, slavery was banned in much of Europe unless the would-be slave was illiterate and had not yet converted to Christianity. For the next fifty years, slavery in America was confined to the taking of select native populations to be enslaved as servants in Europe.

The taking of African slaves and transporting them to America began with the Spanish colonies in the 1560s followed by the English who first brought slaves to their Jamestown, Virginia colony in 1619. Slaves were a desirable commodity to the European settlers because they were deemed critical to the establishment of early cash crops such as coffee, cotton, sugar, and tobacco which funded the colonization of America. The slave trade continued until 1819 when U.S. law declared the practice illegal. During the 250 years slave trading was legal, over a million Africans were brought to the United States against their will. During the ensuing years, by the start of the Civil War in 1860, the U.S. slave population grew to over three million.

The Europeans who settled America were devout Christians. They justified their actions by citing Old Testament scripture which told stories of the capture of foreign tribes to be used as slaves and is not once mentioned as a sin in the extensive Mosaic Laws.

Sadly for nearly 250 years, up until the Civil War, slavery was an integral part of our nation's economic and sociological system. Even the founding fathers ignored the issue as they crafted the beautiful prose that became the Declaration of Independence in 1776. In spite of his strong belief in God, Thomas Jefferson, like most of those taking part in the Continental Congress, owned slaves. In fact, records indicate Jefferson owned between 175 and 265 slaves, and that he was a typical slave-owner who enforced discipline on his slaves by whipping and even selling them to other slave-owners for transgressions. While it is true Jefferson freed a handful of slaves, it is also true that those he freed shared his own DNA.

Patrick Henry, who uttered the famous line "give me liberty or give me death" had some interesting thoughts on slavery. Even though he owned slaves and continued to buy them throughout the Revolutionary War, he was quoted as saying the practice was "as repugnant to humanity as it is inconsistent with the Bible and destructive of liberty." However, like Jefferson, his actions did not match his prose. Unlike many of his fellow Virginians, this self-proclaimed Christian never freed a single slave.

This internal conflict between the words of these men and their actions was explained very well by the French philosopher Montesquieu, who is quoted as saying, "It is impossible for us to suppose these creatures to be men, because, allowing them to be men, a suspicion would follow that we ourselves are not Christian."

The Civil War was a turning point on the issue of slavery in America. While the records attempt to place a deeper rift between the two sides by using phrases like "states rights," the question of slavery was the central issue.

The first reason given by South Carolina for secession from the United States was the refusal of non-slavery states to arrest and return run-away slaves to their owners.

Lincoln himself struggled with the idea of slavery. During the famous campaign of 1858 between Abraham Lincoln and Stephen Douglas, the latter, a Democrat, made his position on slavery very clear: "In my opinion this government of ours is founded on the white basis. It was made by the white man, for the benefit of the white man, to be administered by the white men."

Lincoln, on the other hand seemed to vacillate on the issue and during the debate he stated: "I am not, nor ever have I been in favor of bringing about the social and political equality of the white and black races."

The issue of race was clearly the divisive political factor leading up to the Civil War, as the Democratic party proudly declared itself to be the "white man's party."

In school we were taught that the Union forces were victorious, the union was preserved and President Lincoln freed the slaves with the signing of the Emancipation Proclamation in 1863.

However, declarations and proclamations do not necessarily change hearts.

Following the Civil War, Republicans held a two-thirds majority in both Houses of Congress along with the presidency. Without opposition, they passed laws ushering in the Reconstruction Era which provided new opportunities for the newly freed slaves.

New laws temporarily placed the states of the Confederacy under control of the Union Army and took the voting rights away from its citizens. Former slaves, now called freedmen, were given parcels of land formerly held by plantation owners and were enrolled in school for the first time. Radical Republicans—in cooperation with civil rights activists from the North, and Union supporters (Scalawags) from the South and freedmen—took control of the state governments in the former Confederate States. As a result, many public positions within local, state and federal government were given to blacks. Freedmen were also allowed to enlist in the Union Army, which continued to operate the plantations left vacant by the owners. Reconstruction programs were put in place to build schools and railroads. Blacks were even permitted to play professional baseball—well before the emergence of Jackie Robinson. During the Reconstruction period, the public education system was improved and the tax laws were spread more equitably.

Unfortunately the Panic of 1873 hit the economies of the United States and Europe, leading to a worldwide recession which lasted until 1879 and halted most investments in the southern states. By this time southern whites had regained their voting rights leading to a resurgence of the Democratic Party. The democrats of the south were allied with white paramilitary groups who held great hatred toward the black community and, as a result, worked vigorously to rescind the recently enacted freedoms for the freedmen. This led to a time of intense violence against the black community as the idea of equality between the races could not be accepted.

Beginning in the mid-1870s many black schools and churches were burned, and countless teachers were beaten or murdered. In one incident during the summer of 1876, white paramilitary groups killed over 150 blacks in Louisiana alone.

During this period the Christian church was at war with itself concerning the integration of blacks into society. Activities that encouraged the emancipation of blacks were led by some progressive, mostly northern, members of the clergy. The more conservative white southern churches continued to use the Bible to justify hatred and segregation for blacks.

In an interesting contrast, both sides used the Bible to justify their positions. The progressive clergy chose to focus on the Gospel accounts of the stories of Jesus. They spoke of a God who sent his son Jesus, who was most likely a dark skinned Jew to redeem the sins of all men, regardless of color. The Jesus they presented chose to associate with outcasts and lepers and celebrated stories such as that of the Good Samaritan and the woman at the well. He refuted the outdated teachings of Mosaic Laws represented by the "eye-for-an-eye," retaliation for those that offended us, and replaced it with his teaching to turn the other cheek.

In contrast, the conservative churches chose to focus on the more fundamental and judgmental writings from the Old Testament. In particular, the books of Genesis and Exodus which taught the story of creation, the Great Flood, the Tower of Babel, and the purity of God's chosen people.

The impressive gains providing new freedoms for blacks enacted during Reconstruction were soon overridden by new laws and other actions which fueled racial prejudice and segregation. Led by the Democratic Party, which won control of both the House and Senate, laws were soon passed throughout the country restricting the rights of blacks to vote, prohibiting them from jury duty, and forcing them into depressed and segregated areas. With the protection of the local police, white violence against blacks increased dramatically with routine physical assaults and lynchings mostly throughout the south. Knowing that no white jury would convict them, lynch mobs posed for pictures and smiled at the cameras as lifeless bodies of innocent black men hung in front of them.

Successful blacks became attractive targets for attacks and were often driven from their stores or workplaces. Some cities as far north as Warren, Michigan and Appleton, Wisconsin passed "sundown" laws that prohibited blacks from spending the night within the city limits upon penalty of death. These so-called Jim Crow laws, named after a black character in a popular entertainment act, were intended to keep blacks from gaining any social or political standing in society. These laws kept white nurses from administering to black men, forced blacks to sit in the back rows of any public transportation, use separate public restrooms and drinking fountains, and from dining in the same restaurants as whites.

President Woodrow Wilson, a Democrat and former President of Princeton University, was an avowed segregationist and immediately removed all blacks from federal office when he was elected in 1912 and maintained this segregation until his second term ended in 1921.

Both sides in this battle claimed biblical support for their respective positions. This contradiction was magnified by both parties using the same scriptural reference, Acts 17:26, to support their positions.

The anti-segregation movement emphasized Paul's message to the Christians of Athens in the first half of the verse which said: *"From one man he made every nation of men, that they should inhabit the whole earth."*

The segregationists countered this claim by using the second half of the same verse which states: *"and he determined the times set for them and the exact places where they should live."*

The practice of slavery had cemented the idea that people of color were inferior. After the Civil War ended, white southern churches promoted the underlying fear of miscegenation—the mixing of races and the possibility of interracial marriages. The trepidation created by the very thought of a black man speaking to a daughter of a white man was an effective recruiting tool for the segregationist movement which used its churches to disseminate their message. Even the thought of interracial discussions, which they felt could lead to friendship or even marriage filled them with fear. Churches, such as the Southern Baptists recruited evangelists to warn of the evils of mixed marriages using the term "mongrelization" to describe what would happen if the races mixed. This fear was echoed by pro-segregation clergymen and legislators such as the late senator from Alabama, Walter Givhan, who, when commenting on the historic Supreme Court ruling Brown v. Board of Education, which dealt solely with equal education, said: "What is the real purpose of this? To open the bedroom doors of our white women to Negro men."

A pamphlet that circulated at that time called *Racial Facts* warned of: "Negroid blood like the jungle, steadily and completely swallowing up everything."

This argument still circulates today in some fringe Christian groups that teach the greatest form of genocide would be to allow whites to mix with the black or yellow races, still using the term "mongrelization" of the races. Often quotes from Leviticus, Exodus, Psalms, Hosea, or this verse from Deuteronomy 7:3 are used to support this ridiculous claim: *"Do not intermarry with them. Do not give your daughters to their sons or take their daughters for your sons."*

When taken out of context, this verse appears to support the demand for segregation. However, in context it is about God's direction to the Israelites to destroy their enemies when they enter a new territory. God commands that they must *"destroy them totally."* The "them" God is talking about in verse 3 is clarified earlier in verse 1 as meaning the Hittites, Girgashites, Amorites, Canaanites, Perizzites, Hivites, and Jebusites—basically, everyone who is not an Israelite. It has nothing to do with the color of one's skin.

In the 1960s and 70s, leaders of the Civil Rights movement were acutely aware that any discussion of blacks being integrated into society would be viewed as a stepping stone to interracial marriage. As a result they intentionally limited their legal challenges to issues like equal access to colleges, high schools, transportation, and public establishments. To lessen the threat, they went so far as to make certain that the litigants used in their cases were older married men.

In spite of the efforts to eliminate miscegenation from the discussion, the segregationists continued to fan the fear of sexual relations between the races. Even though the landmark Supreme Court case in 1954, *Brown vs. Board of Education,* was exclusively about admittance into a public school, the white conservative churches' resistance was primarily focused on interracial sex.

Throughout this time, those who supported the Civil Rights movement were keenly aware of the need to show God was on their side. Many white southern clergy quietly provided subtle support for the movement, especially those who had worked as missionaries in foreign countries and been exposed to people of color. Almost immediately after the Brown decision the Southern Baptist Convention endorsed the decision as did the National Council of Churches of Christ, the World Council of Churches, and the Synagogue Council of America. Eventually all major denominations endorsed the ruling.

Following this landmark decision, the civil rights movement continued to make slow progress within most Christian communities, though the position of the clergy was typically more progressive than their membership.

In 1957, the Southern Christian Leadership Conference elected twenty-eight-year-old Martin Luther King Jr. as its President. Using the principles of Christianity and the operational techniques of nonviolent confrontation advocated by Gandhi, he began challenging the Jim Crow laws.

On March 7 of 1965, Dr. King led a peaceful march of black activists across the Edmund Pettus Bridge in Selma Alabama. They were brutally attacked by state troopers and local sheriff's deputies and a gang of local men wearing gas masks and armed with clubs. The marchers were brutally beaten while film crews recorded the event. This attack became known as "Bloody Sunday," and was a turning point in the civil rights movement.

Dr. King then invited ministers from across the country to join him in Selma for what was called the Ministers March. The response was immediate and two days later, on March 9, 1965, more than 450 white ministers, priests, nuns, and rabbis assembled in Selma to support the marchers.

One of those that responded was James Reeb, a white Unitarian Universalist minister from Boston, who was attacked and beaten after walking out of a diner in Selma. He died of his wounds two days later.

In locations across the country, people gathered to memorialize James Reeb's death including over 20,000 in Boston and 15,000 in front of the White House which caught the attention of both the President and First Lady, Lyndon and Lady Bird Johnson. On March 15, eight days after the Bloody Sunday, President Johnson went before a joint session of Congress and introduced the Voting Rights Act of 1965 which outlawed discriminatory voting practices which had disenfranchised so many African Americans.

While not marking the end of prejudice and hatred toward people of color, it was a wonderful moment for the American Christian community because people of all races finally stood up to the ingrained injustice of segregation.

It is incumbent on all Christians to continue to stand up for the rights of all. When we hear a derogatory slang term mentioning a minority, when we receive an e-mail or hear a joke that expresses a racist theme, it is important for us, as professed followers of Christ, to express our distaste in a clear and certain voice.

Hatred toward others has gone on long enough in the Christian community. This is not what Jesus taught and not the message of a loving Christ who spent so much of his time in the company of those who were outcasts and downtrodden.

Christ taught us to love our enemies, give to the needy, attend to the sick, and to concentrate our energies on living in a Christ-like manner rather than in judgment of others. The directions for living a Christ-like life are found in Matthew 5:3–11 which are referred to as the Beatitudes. In the Beatitudes Jesus instructs us that blessed are: the poor, those who mourn, the meek, those who hunger, the merciful, the pure of heart, the peacemakers, and the persecuted. The stories in the Gospels reflect that the life of Jesus was based on these simple instructions.

Christ did not teach us to separate ourselves from those who are not like us. He taught us to go to those that are diseased, needy, outcasts, or of different color and reach out to them. Jesus was re-peatedly chastised for keeping company with those in society who could not defend themselves. He didn't avoid those that were not like him or who were in need. Instead he sought them out.

The parable of the Good Samaritan, in Luke 10:30–37, was a perfect example of this. Shortly after Jesus had declared that man should love his neighbor, he was asked what he meant by the word neighbor. Jesus told the story of a Jewish man that was traveling on a road. He is beaten, robbed, and left for dead on the side of the road. Two religious and devout men—the first a priest, the second a Levite—passed by and each man left him for dead. Finally, a Sa-maritan—who is the bitter enemy and despised by the Jews—comes by and treats his wounds, transports him to an inn, and pays the innkeeper for the room and treatment.

The message from Christ is simple and loving, there is no place for prejudice or hatred. Christ warned us about church leaders that distort his message—much as was done for hundreds of years in America. Matthew 7:15 teaches us: *"Watch out for the false prophets. They come to you in sheep's clothing, but inwardly they are fero-cious wolves. By their fruit you will recognize them."*

We must be always vigilant and curious when the Bible is used to promote hatred. You do not speak for God because of your position. Likewise, you are not a messenger for Christ if you distort his teachings.

It is not where you live, who you love, or the color of your skin that makes you Christ-like. Rather it is how you live your life, what you say, and what you think. When Christ was providing an explanation for not fasting he gave us a wonderful lesson in appearances: Matthew 15:11 *"What goes into a man's mouth does not make him unclean, but what comes out of his mouth, that is what makes him unclean."*

We have dealt with ferocious wolves with an unclean message too long. Let's get back to the real message of Christ—that of tolerance. While Paul was not tolerant of the depravity of the Romans and Greeks, he did teach tolerance when he proclaimed: Galatians 3:28 *"There is neither Jew nor Greek, slave nor free, male nor female, for you are all one in Christ Jesus."*

We all know, from the voice that speaks to us in our quietest moments, that it is wrong and contrary to the life of Christ to allow the hatred of prejudice to enter our lives.

11

The American Church Today

According to *The Pew Forum on Religion & Public Life, U.S. Religious Landscape Survey of 2007*, the population of America is currently seventy-eight percent Christian. Of that number, fifty-one percent are Protestant, twenty-four percent Catholic and the remaining three percent are divided between the Mormon, Orthodox Christian, and Jehovah's Witness. Approximately five percent of Americans list themselves as Jewish, Buddhist, Muslim, Hindu, or New Age. The fastest growing group, sixteen percent, list themselves as unaffiliated, with twelve percent saying they believe in "nothing in particular" and the remaining four percent professing to be either atheist or agnostic.

Even within the fifty-one percent listing themselves as Protestant there are significant variations of theologies with twenty-six percent claiming to be evangelical, eighteen percent mainline Christian and seven percent affiliated with an historic black denomination.

The face of Christianity is also changing in our belief in the inerrancy and inspiration of the Bible. A similar Pew Forum survey from 2006 found thirty-five percent of Christians believe the Bible is the actual Word of God and must be taken literally. In contrast, forty-one percent say the Bible is the Word of God but should not be taken literally. The remaining nineteen percent believe the Bible is a sacred book written by men and not the Word of God. This stands in stark contrast to earlier polls that showed many more Americans believing the Bible was to be taken literally.

The diversity of those claiming to be Christian is manifested in disagreements on many other controversial topics. This chapter will explore what Americans believe when it comes to topics that have historically divided the church.

Modern Christian Denominations

The present day American Christian church is divided into four primary groups encompassing many denominations: They are: Catholicism, Mainline Protestantism, Evangelical Protestantism, and Historic Black churches.

The only group that has stayed together within one denomination is the Roman Catholics which make up approximately one quarter of the U.S. population. The biggest changes in the past several decades to affect the teachings of the Catholic Church came as the result of the Second Vatican Council, which was initiated by Pope John XXIII in 1962. The advocates of these sweeping changes instituted by the Council called this an "opening of the windows." As a result of Vatican II the liturgy of worship was made more inclusive by allowing the use of languages other than Latin. It also opened dialogues with Protestant denominations, the Eastern Orthodox Church, and the Anglican Communion.

Mainline Protestants—which include the United Methodists, the largest Lutheran and Presbyterian bodies, Episcopalians, the United Church of Christ and others—have been the most progressive church bodies. These progressive positions have led to many internal squabbles, losses of members, and churches dividing into separate denominations. Starting in the mid-1960s, most mainline Protestant denominations have accepted women into the ministry. Ordination vows have also been loosened with many now allowing openly homosexual pastors and most of the others are well on their way to the acceptance of gays and lesbians into the pastorate.

The evangelical Protestant denominations include the Southern Baptist Convention, the Assemblies of God, the Pentecostal and fundamentalist churches, and many smaller denominations and independent non-denominational churches. These denominations, and loosely affiliated groups, make up over a quarter of the American population and are more conservative both theologically and politically than the historic mainline churches. Few if any evangelical churches have adopted or even openly discussed homosexual ordination and only a handful have accepted women into the ministry.

Historically black denominations include the more traditional African Methodist Episcopal Church (AME) and African Methodist Episcopal Zion Church (AME Zion) along with the more fundamental Church of God in Christ (COGIC). These churches, which were formed as the result of slavery, tend to be more charismatic than white churches and have more influence on their communities in social and political issues. Many have accepted women into the ministry, though few have accepted homosexuals as pastors.

Within each modern Christian denomination are groups on both sides of every political and social issue. This has led to fragmentation, disagreements, and upheaval mirroring society as a whole. Some would say the only thing on which all Christians agree is to disagree.

Confronting Hot Button Issues

While there are few areas of general agreement within modern day Christendom, there are some issues on which churches have had to reach consensus due to changes in society.

One such issue is that of divorce and remarriage. Sadly, more than half of all marriages end in divorce, forcing the church to become more accepting. To do otherwise would result in huge losses in membership.

Other issues, such as prayer in school and the public display of the Ten Commandments, have been legislated in the courts. While these issues are often raised prior to elections every two years, most legal experts considered these issues settled law. It seems very likely that this pattern will be followed in relation to same-sex marriage.

When these cases become settled law, most churches will be forced to accommodate these members also.

Abortion and birth control are still hot button issues in many denominations and show no sign of abating. Most mainline denominations, while clearly not promoting the idea, have accepted those members who have had abortions or use birth control. However, the Catholic Church and most evangelical churches stand firmly against both. This is also the case with stem cell research where most mainline churches are in favor and the Catholics and most evangelical churches oppose it.

One area where most churches now agree is the keeping of Sunday as Sabbath. Begrudgingly, pretty much every church now accepts the commercialization of society including the fact that stores and businesses are open and sports and other activities are now conducted on Sunday. Protesting the scheduling of events or activities on Sunday, which was common into the mid 1980s, is now relatively rare.

Another area of agreement concerns the diversity of worship styles with pretty much every church denomination now allowing casual dress and contemporary music, although within individual congregations these may still be very emotional issues.

Urban and Suburban Churches

As America expanded from the east to the west, churches were established in virtually every community. The planting of so many churches occurred during a time when America was mostly rural. But as people moved to cities, the country has now become overwhelmingly urban and suburban with over eighty percent now living in metropolitan areas.

Most urban churches fall into a couple categories: tall steeple and traditional neighborhood. Tall steeple churches are large urban churches with a noticeable presence both physically, with their classic structures, and through mission, with their many community outreach programs to those in need. Many members of these churches generally do not live near the church and commute from more opulent areas. Often these large churches are bedrocks of their communities and tend to attract those who have an interest in being involved in an organization that has a commitment of helping those in need. These tall steeple churches are typically more progressive theologically than their suburban counterparts.

In contrast to their richer counterparts, older neighborhood churches in urban areas tend to be small, underfunded, with an older membership, and are located in areas where poorer people live. Many urban churches are being closed as members die off with their buildings being repurposed as an art studio, antique shop, restaurant, or other commercial ventures. Those that survive are being changed to more accurately reflect the population in the neighborhood. For instance, a church that was founded to support European immigrant populations of the early 20th Century is changing to support newer immigrants arriving from countries from the Far East, Middle East, and other areas around the globe.

Suburban churches—in contrast to their urban alternatives—have followed the flight of the baby boom generation to the suburbs. Today most growing churches are located in the suburban areas with many achieving large membership numbers resulting in what is commonly called a mega-church. The largest difference between a tall steeple urban church and its suburban counterpart is the focus of the ministry. Suburban churches tend to be driven by programming for its members with only a token involvement in urban ministry. Another distinction theologically and politically, is that most suburban churches tend to be evangelical and conservative as opposed to urban churches which are apt to be mainline and progressive.

Rural Churches

In the last chapter we discussed how the various denominations grew as America was settled and that, during those times, most people lived in rural communities or on farms. As young people became educated they moved from the country to larger metropolitan areas seeking a better life. Rather than follow the children into the suburbs, the historic mainline denominations, such as the United Methodists, Lutherans, and Presbyterians, relied on their existing churches which were mostly located in the center of large metropolitan urban communities in the so-called tall steeple churches. The churches where the children were raised were left with a shrinking, older population. This is one reason the historic mainline denominations have diminished in membership. At the end of World War II, most young families chose to build their homes in the suburbs which were mostly populated by more conservative evangelical churches. These churches were attractive as they offered programming for adults and children with little emphasis on helping the poor, which was the primary message of Jesus.

As a result, the rural countryside is populated with huge numbers of dying small churches while the nearby suburbs are filled with newer churches offering the latest in worship technology, programs for young and old, and dynamic evangelical pastors who are typically more conservative than their country church brethren.

12

The Church of the Future:
Welcome to the Buffet

The future of the American church will most likely mirror society as a whole. Just as Americans are shying away from joining national organizations such as fraternal clubs like the Elks and Lions, organized religion is facing similar challenges. In the not too recent past, people would define their beliefs by stating they were members of a particular denomination. That was because each denomination had its own set of beliefs that were easy for members to know and understand. But as the country has diversified so has organized religion. Someone who is Presbyterian in the north is apt to have beliefs that are polar opposites of a Presbyterian from the south. The same is true of Episcopalians, Lutherans, and Methodists. These denominational organizations have taken on many of the same characteristics as political parties in that members and clergy no longer agree with fellow members on many different social issues.

As a result many believe denominations will continue to decline and be replaced by independent, non-denominational churches. While this may be good from the standpoint of individuality it will also put more of the burden on finding a church on the attendee themselves. Unfortunately this task becomes more difficult as many churches attempt to disguise their true theology. The large church down the street with the great rock band and alluring pastor may be less progressive than the small, quiet congregation meeting in the high school cafeteria.

At the same time, Americans are becoming less monolithic in their beliefs. In the future many believe the "buffet line" approach to religion will continue to grow. This means it will become commonplace for individuals to find a theology that fits their lifestyle and core beliefs even if these beliefs knit together practices from multiple religions. For example, a person may choose to accept Christian dogma in one area of their life while adding Hindu or Muslim practices in other areas. A buffet line of beliefs where people load their belief plate with a little bit of this and a little bit of that.

In addition to combining practices from multiple faiths, people are also choosing to back various practices that would have been shunned in the past. These include the acceptance of homosexuals as pastors, the use of inclusive language when evoking the name of God, and accepting the fact that the Bible is inspired rather than the actual, inerrant word of God.

While many large urban and suburban mega-churches will continue to flourish, smaller churches will continue to close. In place of the small church will be more house-based ministries where individuals will be encouraged to dialogue with one another as they collectively seek meaning in their lives.

Most change will begin with conflict and, as a result, diminish the size of their respective denominations. This change has begun in recent years in the Episcopal Church which voted to accept homosexual pastors and bishops. Because of that change many of their churches left the American denomination in favor of smaller, more conservative Episcopal denominations based in other countries.

During the summer of 2010, the largest Lutheran denomination voted to accept gay clergy. Within days nearly two hundred churches left that denomination and formed a new Lutheran organization that refutes what the mother church voted to accept. From the opposite perspective, some local ministers teach a theology that differs from the official doctrine which creates division within the congregation, resulting in a splinter church being created.

The fracturing of the well-recognized name brand denominations will continue resulting in weak national organizations replaced by large, well-funded churches that are either a part of a loosely organized group or truly independent of any larger organization.

This has been made possible by technology that allows a church to form a loose relationship with like-minded churches in order to replace the services once provided by a denomination such as a pension fund for pastors, connections with theological seminaries, and administrative rules and regulations that help a church through personnel and property issues.

Modern communications and the Internet have allowed churches to become more independent. This means fewer churches will depend on denominational structures. As this independence grows they will become less willing to accept the dogma and edicts that come from higher ups within organizations. This trend, which started within the mainline denominations, in the future will affect evangelical churches and even the Catholic Church. Historic black denominations, due to their importance within the African American community, may first experience a loss in their membership before seeing changes in their organizational structures. These changes will be driven by more interracial families, changes within neighborhoods and improvements in finances as they relate to other races.

History is always a guide to the future. Over the past several hundred years, as the human condition has improved, the church has continued to lose its influence on society. It appears very likely this trend will continue. The church, which once controlled governments, will grow in number of worldwide adherents however its influence on national politics will diminish.

While the influence of the organized church is negated, the growth of issue-oriented religious nonprofits will increase. These so-called "para-church" organizations are raising huge sums of money and deploying their resources, in laser-like fashion, to support their missions. The para-churches include organizations that help the poor such as World Vision, those that tout family values like Focus on the Family, and religious political action groups such as the Christian Coalition. More and more, the money that was traditionally given in the name of religion is going to these organizations and not to the denominations. With money comes power so it stands to reason those who raise the most will have access to political leaders, and with that comes real power.

Key to the survival of church institutions will be their willingness to accept the role of spiritual leadership without requiring political dominance. While that will be difficult for church leaders to accept, it will become the new reality of religious power in America.

13

Where Does That Leave Us?

There comes a time in each person's life when they must deal, in one way or another, with the issue of faith. How someone deals with faith depends, in part, with one's upbringing and life experiences. It also is important to strip away the veneer of organized religion and actually study the origins and meaning of Scripture. When studying the Bible it is important to answer the following questions about faith and religion: Does your religion require you to accept the belief in an inerrant Bible? Is organized religion the only option for someone wanting to practice their faith? Did Jesus intend for his followers to be members of a church?

In the earlier chapters we have addressed many issues involving religion, faith, and the inerrancy of the Bible.

For myself I do not believe the Bible is divinely inspired or infallible. I also do not believe in the story of creation, the concept of original sin, the virgin birth, or the coming apocalypse.

What does that leave us?

It leaves us with a wonderful story written nearly 2000 years ago by several writers telling how Jesus of Nazareth completely changed the way they lived their lives.

The critical time in the story of Jesus was during his active ministry which lasted approximately three years.

Unfortunately, we have no original documents from this period. In fact, Christ's life and death did not even merit notes in the extensive written records of the Roman Empire.

Following the Words of Jesus

We don't know exactly what Jesus said, or what was said to him.

Quoting these error-filled and contradictory texts verbatim, as if spoken directly by God, diminishes our appreciation for his power and majesty. A God great enough to create such a magnificent universe that was interested in recording his thoughts would make certain that these words were preserved and recorded in various languages, without error.

The errors, omissions, and conflicts presented in the biblical writings are reflective of an honest attempt by writers to share the impact of Jesus with future generations.

The most critical time in the development of the Christian faith was the period immediately following the crucifixion. At that time, somewhere between fifteen and twenty-five men and women, followers of Jesus, at the risk of their lives, gathered to share their experiences with Jesus.

This handful of early believers were unknowingly spreading the seeds of a new religion. These uneducated—most, if not all, illiterate—and unorganized people left the comfort of their homes to travel by foot, from village to village, to share the message of Jesus. There is no reason to believe they were charismatic speakers, instead they were common fishermen and day laborers who possessed a story they could not keep to themselves. The reason this story spread so widely was due to the life Jesus led and not based on the charisma of the disciples.

In contrast, when we study the cults that have developed throughout history, it is the charismatic personality of one individual that is the driving force and not the message being delivered. When a cult leader dies, so does the movement. Without the leader's charisma its followers cannot sustain the energy that drove the movement in the first place.

Jesus must have commanded a presence unlike any ever witnessed. Followers talked about his aura, how he commanded attention and even led people to leave their homes to follow him.

Even Mary, his mother, who by some accounts had several children after Jesus, joined his brother James and left everything to follow him.

After Jesus was crucified, this small band of leaderless men and women formed a movement that followed his teachings, repeating his stories and lessons. Although their presentation lacked the compelling presence of Jesus, his message shown through as the disciples paraphrased the message of Jesus in spite of their inadequacies.

The disciples were adept at matching the story to their audience. If, for instance, they were attempting to convert the Jewish community, like the author of Matthew, they would slant the story to the fulfillment of the Torah. If they were speaking to the gentile community, such as John, they would place more blame on the Jews for the death of Jesus.

We don't know exactly what these first disciples actually said but we do have what writers penned decades later shortly after the Romans had destroyed the temple at Jerusalem. At that time the Christian community was scattered and comprised of hundreds of small groups, each with a slightly different story of Jesus.

Today we continue to ask the question, "What did Jesus actually say?" Nobody really knows for sure. However, using the rules of biblical scholars, we can return to the Bible to find the passages that most likely represented what Jesus said and did. The short phrases, the radical departures from tradition, the parables and stories that would be memorable probably reflect something very close to the words Jesus spoke.

For example, in Mark 12:27, Jesus states: *"He is not the God of the dead, but of the living."*

This verse is contrary to the standard concept of heaven. It is easy to remember and repeat, and something listeners could retell. It is logical to believe Jesus said it or something very similar to it. The verse is also consistent with Luke 17:20–21 that states: *"The kingdom of God does not come with your careful observation. Nor will people say, 'Here it is,' or 'There it is,' because the kingdom of God is within you."*

Why does one have to wait to die to experience heaven? God is for the living and the kingdom of heaven is within you. The concept that greater things await you after you die is to denigrate the beauty of God that is within and around us every minute.

We enter the kingdom of God when we are like children and question everything.

In Mark 10:15 and Luke 18:17, Jesus says: *"I tell you the truth, anyone who will not receive the kingdom of God like a little child will never enter it."*

When we look at the life of Christ, he questioned every dogma of the Jewish faith. Jesus refused to fast, which was strict church dogma. He harvested food and healed the sick on the Sabbath, because rules of the Sabbath didn't make any sense. When Jesus refused to wash his hands, as required by Jewish law, he failed to honor one of the basic practices of Judaism even though he reportedly taught in the synagogue.

As for Jewish practices, there are no references of Jesus ever performing the required sacrifices of Mosaic Law.

In Genesis, Exodus, Numbers, and Deuteronomy, God told Moses and his people exactly what to sacrifice for a particular uncleanly act and exactly how to perform the ritual. The concept of sacrifice was so important that God directed Abraham to sacrifice his own son Isaac, which Abraham was willing to do.

However, Jesus was unwilling to participate in any sacrifice or reinforce any of the Mosaic Laws. This is in stark contrast with many Christians who defend these practices by quoting from the Old Testament.

There is one reported instance of Jesus losing his temper. This involved the overturning of the tables at the temple, which is found in slightly different versions in all four Gospels. In the Gospels Jesus enters Jerusalem and finds people in the temple openly exchanging money by selling cattle, sheep, and doves. They were selling the cattle and doves as part of a sacrifice that was required by Jewish law. This was a matter of convenience since many of these people traveled long distances to come to Jerusalem and celebrate the Jewish Passover. Traveling with a sacrificial calf or dove was difficult. It was far more practical to buy the sacrificial animals once they arrived in Jerusalem. Since there was not one standard currency, money changers were necessary to allow people to make their purchases. It was in this context that Jesus overturned the money tables and drove away the animals, saying: *"My house shall be called a house of prayer, but ye have made it a den of thieves."* Matthew 21:13 (KJV)

Was Jesus angry at those selling their goods? It appears more likely his disgust was focused on the leaders of the synagogue for turning their focus away from God.

It is no wonder that Mark reports that the High Priest and other religious leaders—all who were appointed by the Romans—began to plot ways to kill him. Jesus was challenging their precious dogma along with their sources of income and power. He was seen as a heretic who did not follow their religious laws. This is no different from how the church has historically dealt with those it saw as heretics; they must die or be cast out. Even today the church has shown it cannot tolerate those who use facts of science or historical research to reveal errors in the Bible.

Jesus rarely concerned himself with religious laws. Through his actions and words he repeatedly chose human compassion over doctrine. Jesus asked his followers to think beyond church orthodoxy, even if that meant defying the church elders, in order to obey the will of God.

As an example, occasionally on the Sabbath, when Jesus and his disciples were hungry, they would pick grain for their meals even though it went against Mosaic Law. Jesus also disobeyed Mosaic Law when he stopped the stoning of the adulterous woman who was brought to him by church leaders.

At the temple, Jesus became outraged because people were making money at the expense of the poor. How does that differ from televangelists today who thump the Bible to solicit donations from the elderly, sometimes to support their own extravagant lifestyles?

The Jesus we are able to see, through a careful reading of Scripture, spent much of his time providing for those at the edge of society—the poor, the outcasts and the sick.

One story that is often overlooked is found in Mark 5:25-34. It is about the woman who suffered with menstrual bleeding for twelve years. Because Mosaic Law states that a woman is "unclean" during her monthly cycle she became an outcast. In desperation she reached out to touch Jesus' robe. When she did, rather than rebuking her, he healed her.

The parables taught by Jesus are a good example of how he departed from the teachings of the church. These short stories were both easy to remember and to share and probably more accurately reflect the teachings of Jesus.

To find the true Jesus it is best to read the short phrases and parables attributed to him. The simplicity and beauty of the Beatitudes eloquently exemplify the type of brief concise phrases that a follower would remember. Blessed are the poor. Blessed are those who mourn. Blessed are the meek. Blessed are those who hunger. Blessed are the merciful. Blessed are the pure in heart. Blessed are the peacemakers. Blessed are those that are persecuted. They are easy to remember because they stick in our memory and help bring us closer to God.

The Faith of our Founding Fathers

In our own country, Thomas Jefferson, John Adams, and Benjamin Franklin were three of the great thinkers during our country's founding.

While it is common for politicians, pundits, and church leaders to repeat the claim that our founding fathers were Christian, in reality Adams and Franklin were Deists. They both believed in a God although not in the infallibility of the Bible or the divinity of Jesus.

Thomas Jefferson spent a great deal of time thinking about his faith. Like Adams and Franklin, he did not believe in the historical Old Testament, the virgin birth, or the resurrection. Rather, he considered himself a Christian Deist.

In letters to a friend, Dr. Benjamin Rush, he talked about writing down his thoughts concerning religion, and specifically the Gospels. When pushed by Dr. Rush, Jefferson assured him that he would complete the project saying:

"I have a view of the subject which ought to displease neither the rational Christian nor Deist, and would reconcile many to a character they have too hastily rejected. I do not know that it would reconcile the 'genus irritabile vatum' who are all in arms against me. Their hostility is on too interesting ground to be softened."

The reference to the *genus irritabile vatum*, translated as "irritable species of poets," was probably a reference to Martin Luther, who coined the phrase in 1527. Luther used it to describe some of the Protestant followers who disagreed with his teachings and began to espouse a politically radical primitive Christianity with traits strongly critical of secular authority.

Jefferson was a true disciple of Jesus, however he had serious issues with the Gospels as reflected in his *Syllabus of an Estimate of the Merit of the Doctrines of Jesus Compared with Those of Others* which he sent to Dr. Rush. In it Jefferson wrote of Jesus and the Gospels:

"Hence the doctrines which he really delivered were defective as a whole, and fragments only of what he did deliver have come to us mutilated, misstated, and often unintelligible.

They have been still more disfigured by the corruptions of schismatising followers, who have found an interest in sophisticating and perverting the simple doctrines he taught by engrafting on them the mysticism of a Grecian sophist, frittering them into subtleties, and obscuring them with jargon...

Notwithstanding these disadvantages, a system of morals is presented to us, which, if filled up in the true style and spirit of the rich fragments he left us, would be the most perfect and sublime that has ever been taught by man."

Obviously, Jefferson was not a fan of the Gospel writers yet he had a love and devotion to the teachings of Jesus. Jefferson also believed, through logic, he could separate the true thoughts of Jesus from the dogma presented by the writers of the Bible. That belief led him to write *The Life and Morals of Jesus of Nazareth*, his version of the Gospels that are often referred to as *The Jefferson Bible*. In his letter to Dr. Rush announcing the completion of his work, Jefferson wrote:

"I have performed this operation for my own use, by cutting verse by verse out of the printed book, and by arranging the matter which is evidently his, and which is as distinguishable as diamonds in a dunghill."

While not sharing the certainty of Jefferson in discerning the true teachings of Jesus, or as he put it, separating the words of Jesus from the "dung" of religion, I share his belief that by reading and studying the Gospels we are capable of finding a moral compass for our lives. As Jefferson stated in the same letter:

"There will be found remaining the most sublime and benevolent code of morals which has ever been offered to man."

In the pages of the Gospels, hidden in the dogma and individual perspective of the authors—which Jefferson described as "groveling authors" with "feeble minds"—Jefferson found a beauty that is available for all to see. He wrote:

"Intermixed with these, again, are sublime ideas of the Supreme Being, aphorisms, and precepts of the purist morality and benevolence, sanctioned by a life of humility, innocence, and simplicity of manners, neglect of riches, absence of worldly ambition and honors, with an eloquence and persuasiveness which have not been surpassed."

In *The Life and Morals of Jesus of Nazareth*, Jefferson compiled sayings and parables from the four Gospels. Jefferson omits the virgin birth, the crucifixion, and every miracle recorded.

The Jesus Seminar

The Jefferson Bible is, in fact, a beautiful compilation of the teachings of Jesus, and is strikingly similar to the work of the Jesus Seminar.

The Jesus Seminar is the collective work of biblical scholars who undertook to separate the dogma injected into the Gospels from the actual teachings of Jesus. Their goal was to answer the question: "What did Jesus really say?" The Jesus Seminar published their findings in three reports: *The Five Gospels, The Acts of Jesus* and *The Gospel of Jesus*.

The Five Gospels is a word-by-word evaluation of the quotations of Jesus in the four Gospels as well as a fifth "Gospel" which is the book of Thomas—another independent source of the sayings of Jesus. Thomas was not included in the "accepted" or canonical books of the Bible because it did not emerge until centuries later. Discovered in 1945 at Nag Hammadi, Egypt, Thomas is considered to be a significant find as it appears to be a fourth independent source of sayings and parables of Jesus. Thomas contains 114 sayings and parables ascribed to Jesus, but omits to mention the virgin birth, the trial, or resurrection.

The work of the Jesus Seminar culminated with the report, *The Gospel of Jesus: According to the Jesus Seminar*. This, like *The Jefferson Bible*, is a scholastic attempt to reduce these five books into one Gospel showing the life of Jesus without adding the dogmatic bias of a particular religion.

It is important to read *The Jefferson Bible*, the work of the Jesus Seminar, or your own Bible without bias while overlooking the obvious attempts to convert you to the authors' viewpoint. This allows one to see the teachings of Christ without the dogma of religion. By doing so one will experience the greatest teacher to ever walk the Earth and, in the process, to rediscover a loving God.

Thomas Jefferson said it best in one of his letters when he wrote, "It is in our lives and not our words that our religion must be read."

Reading the Gospels through New Eyes

The concept of being a Christian without the baggage associated with the accompanying rules or dogma of the church is literally to see Jesus for the first time. This is the Jesus that emerges for me as I read the Gospels through new eyes.

Mark 12:28 reports that a teacher of the law asked Jesus: *"Of all the commandments, which is the most important?"* He is said to respond:

Mark 12:29 *"The most important one is this: Hear, O Israel, the Lord our God, the Lord is one. Love the Lord your God with all your heart and with all your soul and with all your mind and with all your strength. The second is this: Love your neighbor as yourself. There is no commandment greater than these."*

When the teacher replied that Jesus was correct, Jesus told him; *"You are not far from the kingdom of God."*

These are the type of short, radical sayings that would probably be remembered well after the event. Jesus believed that these two commandments were the most important. It is important to note, that the two commandments most important to Jesus are not part of the Ten Commandments. To Jesus, loving God, not fearing him as is directed in the Second Commandment, is the most important commandment. This is immediately followed by the near impossible commandment to love your neighbor as yourself. These two commandments from Jesus would be worthy of display in our courthouses and schools.

The message Jesus delivered was radically different from Mosaic Law, yet Mark reports that the teacher of Hebrew law recognized Jesus was correct. A Jewish rabbi agreed with Jesus that these two commandments were far more important than the other ten that are so revered in both Judaism and Christianity.

Jesus instructed us that these simple rules—love your God and love your fellow man—bring us closer to the kingdom of God. It is this message from Christ that I embrace.

They were such radical departures from the teachings of the Pharisees and prior prophets that the disciples repeated the message over and over. Jesus may not have said those exact words, but I believe it is the message he conveyed while here on Earth.

The message "love your neighbor as yourself" provides us with a goal in life that is both a fulfilling lifestyle and brings us closer to the heaven promised by Jesus. As Jesus told the teacher, understanding the power of the commandment brought him a step closer to the love of God. There are no threats of an eternal hell, no warnings, simply an invitation to experience the power of love.

175

The Disciples Actions Provide Powerful Evidence

This brings me to what I believe is the most powerful evidence of the life and resurrection of Jesus. It is the story of the disciples that is rarely told. As a person of science, when I read a story or witness an event, the actions of all of the people become very important—not just the actions of the main characters. Let's look at what happened immediately after the crucifixion of Jesus.

The disciples had spent three years following and learning from Jesus. He offered them no money, no shelter, nor any prospects of a reward. He simply asked them to "follow me."

Jesus then proceeded to mock the civil and religious leaders telling them everything they were doing, teaching, and believing was wrong. He dared to teach in their place of worship while criticizing their established laws. Jesus disrupted their primary source of income by destroying the marketplace, overturning the tables of the money changers, and releasing the animals. When challenged, he mocked them for their rigid rules. It would not be an exaggeration to say Jesus was disliked and probably hated by the religious leaders.

After Jesus was arrested and sentenced to death, his disciples were afraid that their association with this rabble rouser would put their lives in jeopardy.

In chapter 24 of Luke, he tells how the disciples were gathered together in a small home in Jerusalem following the crucifixion when Jesus appeared to them. Luke reports they were "startled and frightened." Wouldn't anybody be? After all, they had just witnessed his crucifixion and they were co-conspirators in his movement. It was logical to assume that the crowds might be coming for them next.

Then, while huddled together, something miraculous happened which turned this group of trembling men and women into fearless missionaries that left this shack and traveled far and wide in the face of threats and imprisonment to tell the incredible story of Jesus.

What event could transform this group of commoners into evangelists? I believe it was the appearance of Jesus. What else could motivate such a reaction? It is my belief they witnessed the risen Christ. Not as a ghost but in flesh and blood. They had the opportunity to see and feel the holes in his hands and feet, and the gaping spear wound in his chest.

Something miraculous had to have occurred. What could possibly make eleven common laborers along with the rest of those who followed Christ to leave their safe house and go out into an environment and culture that had just claimed your leader to speak of the risen Christ? What could possibly motivate these people to risk their lives to tell Christ's story?

An atheist friend believes that because the disciples were illiterate laborers it is more likely they would be easy to convince due to their following of a "Svengali" who could tell a good parable and mesmerize a crowd.

I concede it is probably easier to convince or mesmerize the ignorant. While these disciples were illiterate, there is no reason to believe that they were ignorant. Education was a luxury typically reserved for the clergy and wealthy at that time, and writing has very little value for a sustenance farmer or fisherman.

History is filled with great storytellers and evangelicals whose mesmerizing speeches swayed multitudes. During the time of Jesus there were many such leaders, among them John the Baptist. While he had a significant following, his followers did not extend beyond his lifetime.

In our own lifetimes there have been charismatic leaders who most now consider madmen; such as Jim Jones, founder of the Peoples Temple, and David Koresh of the Branch Davidians. Both of these men convinced their followers that they were the living Christ. While many of their followers survived the suicidal actions of their leaders, none have effectively recruited devotees following their deaths.

The disciples didn't wait to spread the news of the risen savior, they went out immediately to share the good news. Within a couple hundred years their message had spread throughout the Mediterranean area. They accomplished this without television, no evening news or any other modern communications. Communication was a very tedious and slow process that required travel by foot, finding an audience, and converting listeners. Finally, after approximately fifty years, their stories were written down which is how the sayings and parables of Jesus were recorded. By this time, the Christian community had already spread throughout the region.

The essence of Christianity for me is its message of love, compassion, and kindness that challenges us to be better than we believe possible. It is about striving to do things beyond what we believe is within our capabilities. Can we truly love our neighbors more than ourselves?

Should we have concerns about the Bible containing errors? Is the notion that Christ was born of a virgin all that important to the core of our beliefs?

To me the story that rings true in the anvil of my soul is that Jesus brought us a message from God that guides us to a complete and fulfilling life—a heaven within ourselves. Jesus taught us to forsake the strict dogma of the church, to think for ourselves and live our lives in a morally-guided manner. He taught us to look beyond appearances, a person's station in life, and treat all with respect. He welcomed the woman at the well even though she had several husbands and was living with another man, and showed her kindness and compassion—not disdain and disgust.

His message was so startling to the existing religious leaders that he had to be silenced. These religious leaders couldn't allow independent thought because it threatened their power. Jesus had to be crucified to save mankind from its sins.

And miracle of miracles, wonder of wonders, he arose from the dead. I know he did. Not because it is written in a book but because it is the only logical explanation for me. I picture a terrified group of men and women huddled in that small house following the crucifixion. The screaming of the crowd to crucify Jesus and spare the common criminal was still ringing in their ears. Peter refused, out of fear for his life, to even acknowledge that he knew Jesus. What happened in that house to make them want to leave its security to tell all who would listen about a man named Jesus that was raised from the dead?

For me there is only one explanation. The resurrection is true, Jesus rose from the dead and the disciples saw the living Jesus.

Conclusion:
God is Great, Without Religion

Each of the world's religions has its dark side and Christianity is no exception. Crusades, Inquisitions, witch trials, slavery, segregation, and homophobia have each played a role in driving countless people away from the Christian faith. This begs the question: Has Christianity been a positive or negative influence on mankind?

In his excellent book, *God is Not Great: How Religion Poisons Everything*, author Christopher Hitchens asks similar questions. He concludes that all of the world religions, including Christianity, are without merit. He makes many compelling arguments, however, I feel he is missing some important points.

I believe Christianity has provided a tremendous message of love, optimism, and respect for humankind. Personally, the Christ I met through my exposure to the teachings of Jesus has given me an inner peace and moral compass I doubt would have come to me on my own. I have witnessed selfless acts of moral courage and personal sacrifice that have filled my life with joy and humility. As a child I watched as Harold, my grandfather, provided Christian hospitality to strangers by opening up his doors and giving up his own bed while providing food and sacrificing his own safety, all in the spirit of Jesus.

That said, I agree with the second half of Hitchens' title, "organized" religion has poisoned the message of Christ. It isn't Jesus or Christianity that poisons everything—rather it is religion.

There was nothing poisonous, exclusive, or antagonistic about the life of Christ. He did not encourage the attacks of his followers on the poor, the politicians, or even the Jewish leaders. He lived a simple life in harmony with God and opened his heart and arms to every person he met, regardless of their beliefs. He welcomed the gentiles, the Jews, the poor, and even the rich into his presence professing a better, more God-like way to live.

Following his death and resurrection, his followers spread out across the Mediterranean region telling the wonderful story of a risen loving Christ. The role Paul played in the early church cannot be overestimated. Though I do not condemn Paul's intentions, many interpretations of his writings led to theologies that took away from the pure message of Christ.

Remember, Paul was not a disciple of Jesus and never met him personally. Instead he was converted to Christianity by a vision of Jesus that transformed his life. Paul did not personally hear the sermons or witness the day-to-day life of Jesus. Yet he openly disputed and argued with those who lived with Jesus during his ministry on Earth. Through his intellect and writings, his version of Christianity won out over the verbal messages of the original disciples who, as simple men, lacked formal education.

Paul, while equally as motivated as the disciples, had the distinct advantage of being able to read and write. As Paul traveled from city to city, his message remained constant and often disputed the message from the disciples such as Peter. His writings were mostly in the form of letters such as his letter to the Romans. In them he articulates his vision of Christianity constructed around his understanding of Jesus' message. Paul's letters gave him a tremendous advantage over the disciples who were less educated, not articulate, and lacked organizational skills.

Paul's efforts in Rome were critical to spreading the Christian message throughout Rome and its ultimate embrace by the Roman Emperor, Constantine, a couple hundred years later. This marriage of a growing religion as envisioned by Paul backed by the power and organization of the Roman Empire, eventually created the most powerful theocratic state in history. The combination of the tyrannical, autocratic power of the government with a set of unbending rules, as provided by the Church, gave the Roman government complete control over the population. The obedience required by this combination gave the state control over both the physical and spiritual lives of its subjects while generating a tremendous amount of money for the church.

This was a great lesson to the newly powerful Roman Catholic Church. By taking absolute authority over the Christian population, modeled after the structure of the Roman empire, the church learned very quickly how to control the population.

The Catholic Church traces its history to Peter who it calls its first "pope." This is in conflict with its own history since the office of the papacy was not created until the middle of the second century. The position of pope, also referred to as the "Holy See," provided a unifying force for the multitude of small Christian churches that had launched through the efforts of the disciples. To increase the stature of the pope, the Catholic church declared God selected the pope, through a secret voting process, and that his opinions and decrees were inerrant.

Those disloyal to the emperor were labeled traitors and subject to prosecution. Similarly, anyone not loyal to the church and its pope were deemed heretic and subject to death. When heretics were uncovered, the church and government took their lives and wealth resulting in more converts to Christianity and an increased fortune in the church coffers.

Constantine not only established the first Christian theocracy, he was instrumental in the compilation of the Christian Bible through the actions of the first Council of Nicea in the year 325.

The Church, armed with the support of the Roman Empire and a Bible that was deemed to be inerrant and directly inspired by God that supported their concept of Christianity, led an all out effort to rid the world of non-believers. This extended beyond the fall of the Roman Empire, in the fifth century, and culminated with the Crusades and Inquisitions extending into the thirteenth century. In fact, until the reformed movement of the 1500s, there was no room for anyone who did not become subservient to the pope, and worship as instructed.

Even in America, through the witch trials, slavery, racism, segregation, suppression of women, and failure to accept homosexuals, it is easy to understand why people wonder if Christianity has been a positive influence in the world.

This is not the teaching of Jesus. Clearly, these heinous acts, "holy wars," and discrimination are not in agreement with the teaching of Christ. Instead they are the dogma created by people in the name of religion. It can be argued much of organized religion is about power and money. The tendency is that those with the most money, members and power can prevail over the meek and the modest—those who Jesus defended.

The negative impact of organized religion is also true of nearly all the world's religions. Islam, which portrays itself as a religion of peace, includes fundamentalist groups responsible for airline hijackings, suicide bombers, and even American homegrown terrorism purportedly carried out by Nidal Malik Hasan, a U.S. Army Major at Fort Hood, Texas. The reported shouts of "Allah Akbar" or "Allah is Great" by those committing these atrocities demonstrates the strong influence of religion on their actions.

While it is easy to blame the religion of Islam for the actions of its extremists, do we show equal disdain for fanatical Christianity that motivated the shooter at the Holocaust Museum or the person who executed the abortion doctor in Wichita, Kansas while he was ushering at his church?

Though our recent wars in the Middle East were not intended as an attack on heretics, during the invasion of Iraq, America's evangelical President made the mistake of referring to the war on terror as a "crusade." To add to the fire, one of our Generals declared that the wars in the Middle East were wars between Christianity and Islam and that his troops would triumph over his adversary because "I knew my God was bigger than his. I knew that my God was a real God and his was an idol." Quotes that remind us of a popular hymn that is still sung frequently in Evangelical services, titled "Onward

Christian Soldiers," written in the nineteenth century and embraced by the Salvation Army:

> *Onward Christian soldiers, marching as to war,*
> *With the cross of Jesus going on before.*

Given the bloody history of Christianity along with the recent words of many of our leaders, it is easy to see why even moderates in the Muslim world see the American incursions in the Middle East as a holy war.

As a nation, and as individuals, we must guard against the belief that our actions, based on fundamental Christian doctrine, are correct and just. Because America is a mostly Christian nation does not mean all our actions are right or automatically make us the good guys. Abraham Lincoln warned against such egotism when he stated: "Our task should not be to invoke religion and the name of God by claiming God's blessing and endorsement for all our national policies and practices—saying, in effect, that God is on our side. Rather, we should pray and worry earnestly whether we are on God's side."

I recently listened to a sermon where the minister was talking about climate change. He mentioned the destruction that would be caused if this trend, which he doubted, continued. He stated Christians should not worry about this devastation but rather should embrace it, as this may be the end of times as foreseen in the book of Revelation. From my perspective, this is much like the philosophy of the suicide bombers. Any religion that teaches that your actions here on Earth are simply preparation for an eternity of "bliss" is at risk of committing atrocities in the name of God. Blaise Pascal, the sixteenth century French philosopher expressed it so accurately when he stated: "Men never do evil so completely and cheerfully as when they do it from religious conviction."

There is nothing wrong with believing in an eternal heaven, unless you disregard your moral obligations while here on Earth. Jesus spoke often of the "kingdom of God," but he took a great amount of time to instruct us how to act while here on Earth. The commandments to love God, love your neighbor as yourself, and to love your enemies would preclude such a reprehensible response.

The many good acts performed by people throughout the world are often offset by the desire of many religions to eliminate all competitors, even those within Christian denominations. How do we dare dream of reaching religious tolerance when so-called people of faith seem determined to carry on wars and other acts of hatred against those who do not agree with their religious beliefs?

While I agree with the subtitle of the Christopher Hitchens' book, I strongly disagree with the title, *God Is Not Great.*

I can see why many people would believe this. If you believe in a God of limited power then it stands to reason that God does not exist as advertised by the church.

However, when you witness the incredible journey that this universe has traveled and continues to travel with the multitude of solar systems each uniquely magnificent, it seems completely inconceivable that there isn't some higher being involved. When you contemplate the transformations that have occurred over millions of years that have changed the smallest life forms into the miracle of the human being, the idea of a "master plan" becomes more feasible to the human mind than the idea of all this occurring simply by "chance."

When we marvel at the beauty of the majestic snow covered mountains, the delicate intricacy of a spider web, and the completeness we feel from being loved, that is when we feel the presence of God. A God so great that even our greatest thinkers can't possibly comprehend his form or majesty.

I understand that the introduction of a Creator into the Theory of Evolution is unnecessary and contrary to good science. Scientists would correctly remind us that the idea of God does not enhance the scientific theory.

On a personal basis, I disagree. My belief in God adds to the miracle of evolution, the majesty of the universe, the intricacy of the human body, and to our presence here on Earth. For this reason, sound scientific theories and the belief in God are not mutually exclusive. There is no reason why believing in God precludes someone from also accepting good science.

Though atheists will surely not convert to accepting the existence of God because of my writing, I would challenge them to entertain the possibility, not based on scientific evidence, but rather on a personal experience. I offer no further proof other than fullness I feel when I close my eyes and open my heart to God's guidance. I don't pretend to hear verbal directions, however I feel a love encompassing me that provides a moral path and a oneness to the wonders that is life.

To my friends and family who attend church, I know your faith community provides comfort, fellowship, and a sense of belonging. I pray that God, and the presence of God, is never lost due to church dogma. Subsequently, I hope this book has provided a new perspective on organized religion and God. I encourage you to open your mind to the research that guides my perspective, but not at the expense of your faith which has guided you throughout the years.

Worshiping Christ without the encumbrances of church dogma allows us to see the Jesus who motivated those twenty-five disciples to travel throughout the known world to tell a story of love, and the way to find the kingdom of God here on Earth. Heaven is within every one of us. Listen to your Holy Spirit and the love of God to enjoy every second of this miracle that is life here on Earth.

They actually do make Christians like my Grandfather Harold today. However their voices are often drowned out by those who preach hate and division.

May God bless you always, and may he bless your own journey of faith.

Suggested Reading

The following books have been instrumental to my research:

Holy Bible	King James Version
Holy Bible	New International Version
A Short History of Nearly Everything	Bill Bryson
The Jefferson Bible	Thomas Jefferson
The Five Gospels	Funk, Hoover, and the Jesus Seminar
The Gospel of Jesus: According to the Jesus Seminar	Robert Funk and the Jesus Seminar
Jesus for the Non-Religious	John Shelby Spong
The Jesus I Never Knew	Philip Yancey
God Is Not Great	Christopher Hitchens
Jesus Interrupted	Bart D. Ehrman
God's Problem	Bart D. Ehrman
Misquoting Jesus	Bart D. Ehrman
Lost Christianities	Bart D. Ehrman
The Seeker's Guide	Elizabeth Lesser
The Call to Conversion	Jim Wallis
The Authentic Gospel of Jesus	Geza Vermes
The Gospel of the Flying Spaghetti Monster	Bobby Henderson
The Battle for God	Karen Armstrong
Religious Literacy	Stephen Prothero
God's Politics	Jim Wallis
Who Wrote the New Testament	Burton L. Mack
The Greatest Show on Earth	Richard Dawkins
God: the Evidence	Patrick Glynn
Jesus: An Historian's Review of the Gospels	Michael Grant
He Still Moves Stones	Max Lucado
The Applause of Heaven	Max Lucado
No Wonder They Call Him the Savior	Max Lucado
A Gentle Thunder	Max Lucado
When God Whispers Your Name	Max Lucado

About the Author

Vern Jones was raised in rural Michigan by a very devout evangelical family whose faith involved daily Bible reading. As he reached his early teens, his interest in the sciences created internal conflict between the inerrant word of God, as taught by his faith, and the laws of nature. This conflict ultimately led to his leaving the church, rejecting an opportunity to go into the ministry, and pursuing an education in the sciences.

While raising a family and founding three successful businesses, he felt emptiness from the absence of inner resolution regarding his place on this Earth, and what role, if any, God played in his life. This need to find a faith that resonated led him to explore other faith traditions. As he witnessed the comfort each faith provided to the faithful, none seemed to resonate with him as much as the story of Jesus.

After numerous unfulfilling experiments with various Christian denominations, his studies brought him to the writings on the life of Jesus by Thomas Jefferson. The idea of a faith in Christ without the miracles, without the condemnations, and without the church building dogma initiated a decades-long self study project to determine the origins of the Bible, the influence of the church on this incredible story, and an effort to find a faith he could own.

Vern is not the product of a seminary; he is not attempting to convert you to his personal beliefs, but simply a seeker, like many of you, who has taken the time to share his journey in the hope that it helps you find a faith that rings true in your soul.

CPSIA information can be obtained at www.ICGtesting.com
Printed in the USA
BVOW04s1952200514

354054BV00005B/33/P